There Is A Season

There Is A Season

An Inspirational Journal

Robert F. Morneau

with photographs by Aaron J. Walschinski, O. Praem.

Prentice-Hall, Inc.
Englewood Cliffs, New Jersey

Prentice-Hall International, Inc., *London*
Prentice-Hall of Australia, Pty. Ltd., *Sydney*
Prentice-Hall Canada, Inc. *Toronto*
Prentice-Hall of India Private Ltd., *New Delhi*
Prentice-Hall of Japan, Inc., *Tokyo*
Prentice-Hall of Southeast Asia Pte. Ltd., *Singapore*
Whitehall Books, Ltd., *Wellington, New Zealand*
Editora Prentice-Hall do Brasil Ltda., *Rio de Janeiro*

© 1984 by
Prentice-Hall, Inc.
Englewood Cliffs, N.J.

Library of Congress Cataloging in Publication Data

Morneau, Robert F.
  There is a season.

  Bibliography: p.
  1. Quotations, English.   2. Literary
calendars.   I. Title.
PN6081.M57   1984   082   84–11622

ISBN 0-13-914755-1
ISBN 0-13-914706-3 {PBK}

Printed in the United States of America

PREFACE

Behind the abandoned barn stood an old, long-handled pump—rusty, unused, and ignored. Years before, when the barn graciously housed cattle and was laden with the fall harvest, the pump enjoyed great popularity as it served plants, animals, and man with its pure, cool, nourishing gift. Not so now! Years of aridity raised the question of its total demise. I had to investigate. Finding a small bucket I returned to my old friend and, recalling that fine art of priming, began to call forth the pump's deepest treasure. Within twenty minutes, after considerable resistance and a stream of brown, rusty water, one might have said that the pump had merely taken a short nap and was now in its prime of life. Pure, fresh water flowed in abundance and, though plants and animals had long gone, I once again tasted life.

This journal is a primer, its goal—to stimulate thought and feeling about a variety of life experiences. What is life? Where does evil reside? How do I deal with time? Who is God? Self? Why the mystery of death? Whence desire? Each month begins with a poem and a series of reflections, questions, and lessons. A theme for each week is followed by various quotations concerning that particular theme. A scriptural reference is suggested to help the reader interpret the quotes from the perspective of faith. A space is then provided to note a thought, a feeling, or a call to action that might surface in one's mind or heart. If the priming has gone well, the space to write the reflection will probably be too limited.

Though the journal is set up chronologically, it may well happen that a given theme does not resonate with immediate experience. In that case, the reader would be well advised to forget about the monthly structure and turn to any selection of the calendar and ponder those quotations and scriptural texts that speak to the moment. Further, the selection of biblical references is somewhat arbitrary; I saw an association between the quotation and the reference; you may not. So be it! What is essential is that we do not waste our lives—becoming rusty, unused, dried up. We are made instruments of God by the baptismal water that once flowed on our heads and in our hearts. We hope to keep that stream alive.

Robert F. Morneau

ACKNOWLEDGMENTS

The author acknowledges the generous assistance of many friends who made this book possible. Deserving special mention are:

Sister Mary de Sales Hoffman, O.S.F. and Sister Marie Isabel McElrone, O.S.F. for editing the manuscript;

Rosemary Bomberg and Bonnie Wiegert for typing.

The Divine Comedy, by Dante Alighieri, translated by Lawrence Grant White. Copyright 1948 by Pantheon Books, Inc. Selections reprinted with permission of Pantheon Books, a division of Random House, Inc.

The Confessions of St. Augustine, translated by John K. Ryan. Copyright 1960 by Doubleday and Company, Inc. Selections reprinted by permission of Doubleday and Company, Inc.

Beowulf: The Oldest English Epic, translated by Charles W. Kennedy. Copyright 1940 by Oxford University Press, Inc.; renewed 1968 by Charles W. Kennedy. Selections reprinted by permission of Oxford University Press, Inc.

The Diary of a Country Priest, by Georges Bernanos. Translation copyright 1937, and renewed 1965 by Macmillan Publishing Co., Inc. Selections reprinted by permission of Macmillan Publishing Co., Inc.

Francis: The Journey and the Dream, by Murray Bodo. Copyright 1972 by St. Anthony Messenger Press. Selections reprinted by permission of St. Anthony Messenger Press.

A Man for All Seasons, by Robert Bolt. Copyright 1960, 1962, by Robert Bolt. Selections reprinted by permission of Random House, Inc.

Pointing the Way, by Martin Buber, translated by Maurice S. Friedman. Copyright 1957 by Martin Buber. Selection reprinted by permission of Schocken Books, Inc.

Resistance, Rebellion and Death, by Albert Camus, translated by Justin O'Brien. Copyright 1960 by Alfred A. Knopf, Inc. Selections reprinted by permission of the publisher.

Witness, by Whittaker Chambers. Copyright 1952 by Whittaker Chambers. Selections reprinted by permission of Random House, Inc.

The Everlasting Man, by G. K. Chesterton. Copyright 1925 by Dodd, Mead and Co., Inc. Selections reprinted by permission of Dodd, Mead and Co., Inc., and Miss D. E. Collins.

Orthodoxy, by G. K. Chesterton. Copyright 1908, 1936, by Dodd, Mead and Co., Inc. Selection reprinted by permission of Dodd, Mead and Co., Inc., and Miss D. E. Collins.

Saint Francis of Assisi, by G. K. Chesterton. Copyright 1924 by George H. Doran Co. Selections reprinted by permission of Miss D. E. Collins.

St. Thomas Aquinas, by G. K. Chesterton. Copyright 1933 by Sheed and Ward. Selections reprinted by permission of Andrews and McMeel, Inc.

Transcendent Selfhood: The Rediscovery of the Inner Life, by Louis Dupré. Copyright 1976 by The Seabury Press, Inc. Selections reprinted with permission of The Seabury Press, Inc.

The Night Country, by Loren Eiseley. Copyright 1971 by Loren Eiseley. Selections reprinted by permission of Charles Scribner's Sons.

I Will Be Called John, by Lawrence Elliott. Copyright 1973 by Lawrence Elliott. Selections reprinted by permission of Reader's Digest Press.

A Passage to India, by E. M. Forster. Copyright 1924 by Harcourt Brace Jovanovich, Inc.; renewed 1952 by E. M. Forster. Selections reprinted by permission of the publisher.

"Stripped Tree," from *Some Did Return,* by Ruth Mary Fox. Copyright 1976 by Ruth Mary Fox. Selection reprinted by permission of Wake-Brook House.

The Poetry of Robert Frost, edited by Edward Connery Lathem. Copyright 1923, 1930, 1934, 1939, 1969, by Holt, Rinehart and Winston. Copyright 1936, 1951, 1958, 1962, by Robert Frost. Copyright 1967 by Lesley Frost Ballantine. Selections reprinted by permission of Holt, Rinehart and Winston, Publishers.

C. S. Lewis: A Biography, by Roger Lancelyn Green and Walter Hooper. Copyright 1974 by Roger Lancelyn Green and Walter Hooper. Selection reprinted by permission of Harcourt Brace Jovanovich, Inc.

When the Well Runs Dry, by Thomas Green, S.J. Copyright 1979 by Ave Maria Press. Selection reprinted by permission of Ave Marie Press.

The Life of Faith, by Romano Guardini, translated by John Chapin. Copyright 1961 by the Newman Press. Selections reprinted by permission of Paulist Press.

The Living God, by Romano Guardini, translated by Stanley Godman. Copyright 1957 by Pantheon Books, Inc. Selection reprinted by permission of Pantheon Books, a division of Random House, Inc.

The Lord, by Romano Guardini, translated by Elinor Castendyk Briefs. Copyright 1954 by Henry Regnery Company. Selection reprinted by permission of Regnery Gateway, Inc.

Siddhartha, by Herman Hesse, translated by Hilda Rosner. Copyright 1951 by New Directions Publishing Corporation. Selections reprinted by permission of New Directions.

A Distant Trumpet, by Paul Horgan. Copyright 1951, 1952, 1953, 1954, 1960, by Paul Horgan. Selections reprinted by permission of Farrar, Straus and Giroux, Inc.

Memories of the Future, by Paul Horgan. Copyright 1966 by Paul Horgan. Selections reprinted by permission of Farrar, Straus and Giroux, Inc.

The Reed of God, by Caryll Houselander. Copyright 1944 by Sheed and Ward. Selections reprinted by permission of Andrews and McMeel, Inc.

Hind's Feet on High Places, by Hannah Hurnard. Copyright 1977 by Tyndale House Publishers, Inc. Selections reprinted by permission of Tyndale House Publishers, Inc.

Hedda Gabler, from *Eleven Plays of Henrik Ibsen,* translated by Gosse and Archer. Selections reprinted by permission of Random House, Inc.

The Complete Works of St. John of the Cross, translated by Kieran Kavanaugh, O.C.D., and Otilio Rodriguez, O.C.D. Copyright 1964 by Washington Province of Discalced Carmelites, Inc. Selections reprinted by permission of ICS Publications.

Julian of Norwich, translated by Edmund Colledge, O.S.A., and James Walsh, S.J., from The Classics of Western Spirituality Series. Copyright 1978 by the Missionary Society of St. Paul the Apostle in the State of New York. Selections reprinted by permission of Paulist Press.

Memories, Dreams, Reflections, by C. G. Jung, translated by Richard and Clara Winston. Translation copyright 1961, 1962, 1963 by Random House, Inc. Selections reprinted by permission of Pantheon Books, a division of Random House, Inc.

The Healing Touch of Affirmation, by Thomas Kane. Copyright 1976 by House of Affirmation, Inc. Selection reprinted by permission of Affirmation Books.

The Decline of Pleasure, by Walter Kerr. Copyright 1962 by Walter Kerr. Selections reprinted by permission of Simon & Schuster.

Philosophical Fragments, by Sören Kierkegaard, translated by David Swenson. Copyright 1936. Copright 1962 by Princeton University Press. Selections reprinted by permission of Princeton University Press.

The Four Loves, by C. S. Lewis. Copyright 1960 by Helen Joy Lewis. Selections reprinted by permission of Harcourt Brace Jovanovich.

The Great Divorce, by C. S. Lewis. Copyright 1946 by Macmillan Publishing Co., Inc., renewed 1974 by Alfred Cecil Harwood and Arthur Owen Barfield. Selections reprinted by permission of Macmillan Publishing Co., Inc. and William Collins Sons & Co., Ltd.

A Grief Observed, by C. S. Lewis. Copyright 1961 by N. W. Clerk. Selections reprinted by permission of The Seabury Press, Inc.

The Horse and His Boy, by C. S. Lewis. Copyright 1954 by C. S. Lewis Pte. Ltd. Copyright renewed. Selections reprinted by permission of Macmillan Publishing Co., Inc., and William Collins Sons & Co., Ltd.

The Magician's Nephew, by C. S. Lewis. Copyright 1955 by C. S. Lewis. Selections reprinted by permission of The Bodley Head.

Mere Christianity, by C. S. Lewis. Copyright 1943, 1945, 1952, by Macmillan Publishing Co., Inc. Copyrights renewed. Selections reprinted by permission of Macmillan Publishing Co., Inc., and William Collins Sons & Co., Ltd.

Out of the Silent Planet, by C. S. Lewis. Copyright 1965 by C. S. Lewis. Selections reprinted by permission of The Bodley Head.

Perelandra, by C. S. Lewis. Copyright 1944 by C. S. Lewis. Selections reprinted by permission of The Bodley Head.

The Screwtape Letters, by C. S. Lewis. Copyright 1942 by C. S. Lewis. Copyright renewed. Selections reprinted by permission of Macmillan Publishing Co., Inc., and William Collins Sons & Co., Ltd.

The Silver Chair, by C. S. Lewis. Copyright 1953 by C. S. Lewis Pte. Ltd. Copyright renewed. Selections reprinted by permission of Macmillan Publishing Co., Inc., and William Collins Sons & Co., Ltd.

Surprised by Joy, by C. S. Lewis. Copyright 1955 by C. S. Lewis. Selections reprinted by permission of Harcourt Brace Jovanovich, Inc.

That Hideous Strength, by C. S. Lewis. Copyright 1946 by C. S. Lewis. Selections reprinted by permission of The Bodley Head.

Till We Have Faces, by C. S. Lewis. Copyright 1956 by C. S. Lewis. Selections reprinted by permission of Harcourt Brace Jovanovich, Inc.

The Voyage of the Dawn Treader, by C. S. Lewis. Copyright 1952 by C. S. Lewis Pte. Ltd. Copyright renewed. Selections reprinted by permission of Macmillan Publishing Co., Inc., and William Collins Sons & Co., Ltd.

The Weight of Glory and Other Addresses, by C. S. Lewis. Copyright 1949 by Macmillan Publishing Co., Inc., renewed 1977 by Arthur Owen Barfield. Selection reprinted by permission of Macmillan Publishing Co., Inc.

Babbitt, by Sinclair Lewis. Copyright 1922 by Harcourt Brace Jovanovich, Inc. Copyright 1950 by Sinclair Lewis. Selections reprinted by permission of Harcourt Brace Jovanovich, Inc.

A Gift From the Sea, by Anne Morrow Lindbergh. Copyright 1955 by Anne Morrow Lindbergh. Selections reprinted by permission of Pantheon Books, a division of Random House, Inc.

The Integrating Mind, by William Lynch. Copyright 1962 by Sheed and Ward. Selection reprinted by permission of Andrews and McMeel, Inc.

The Scarlet Letter: Text, Sources, Criticism, by Kenneth S. Lynn. Copyright 1961 by Harcourt Brace Jovanovich, Inc. Selections reprinted by permission of the publisher.

Raïssa's Journal, presented by Jacques Maritain. Copyright 1963 by Desclée De Brouwer. Translation copyright 1974 by Magi Books, Inc. Selections reprinted by permission of Magi Books, Inc.

Saint-Watching, by Phyllis McGinley. Copyright 1961, 1962, 1965, 1967, 1968, 1969 by Phyllis McGinley. Selections reprinted by permission of Viking Penguin, Inc.

Meister Eckhart, translated by Raymond Bernard Blakney. Copyright 1941 by Harper and Row, Inc. Selection reprinted by permission of Harper & Row, Publishers, Inc.

Moby Dick, by Herman Melville. Copyright 1950 by Random House, Inc. Selections reprinted by permission of Random House, Inc.

The Seven Storey Mountain, by Thomas Merton. Copyright 1948 by Harcourt Brace Jovanovich, Inc.; renewed 1976 by The Trustees of the Merton Legacy Trust. Selections reprinted by permission of the publisher.

Poverty of Spirit, by Johannes B. Metz. Copyright 1968 by The Missionary Society of St. Paul the Apostle in the State of New York. Selection reprinted by permission of Paulist Press.

Collected Poems, by Edna St. Vincent Millay. Copyright 1923, 1951 by Edna St. Vincent Millay and Norma Millay Ellis. Selection reprinted by permission of Norma Millay Ellis.

Utopia, by Sir Thomas More, translated and edited by Robert Adams. Copyright 1975 by W. W. Norton and Co., Inc. Selections from Book 2 reprinted by permission of W. W. Norton and Company, Inc.

We Hold These Truths, by John Courtney Murray. Copyright 1960 by Sheed and Ward. Selections reprinted by permission of Andrews and McMeel, Inc.

The Word: Readings in Theology, by Karl Rahner *et al.,* compiled at the Canisianum, Innsbruck. Copyright 1964 by Macmillan Publishing Co., Inc. Selection reprinted by permission of Macmillan Publishing Co., Inc.

Growth in the Spirit, by François Roustang, S.J., translated by Kathleen Pond. Copyright 1963 by Sheed and Ward. Selections reprinted by permission of Andrews and McMeel, Inc.

The Little Prince, by Antoine de Saint-Exupéry. Copyright 1943, 1971, by Harcourt Brace Jovanovich, Inc. Selections reprinted by permission of the publisher.

The Awful Rowing Toward God, by Anne Sexton. Copyright 1975 by Loring Conant, Jr., Executor of the Estate of Anne Sexton. Reprinted by permission of Houghton Mifflin Company.

Passages, by Gail Sheehy. Copyright 1974, 1976, by Gail Sheehy. Selection reprinted by permission of E. P. Dutton, Inc.

Christology at the Crossroads, by Jon Sobrino, S.J., translated by John Drury. Copyright 1978 by Orbis Books. Selections reprinted by permission of Orbis Books.

"A World Split Apart," address given at Harvard University, June, 1978, by Aleksandr Solzhenitsyn. Selection reprinted by permission of Harper & Row.

The Grapes of Wrath, by John Steinbeck. Copyright 1939 by John Steinbeck. Copyright renewed 1967 by John Steinbeck. Selections reprinted by permission of Viking Penguin, Inc.

Paradise Restored, by Don Taylor. Selection reprinted with permission of Margaret Ramsey, Ltd.

The Complete Works of St. Teresa of Jesus, Vol. 1, translated and edited by E. Allison Peers. Copyright 1944 by Sheed and Ward. Selections reprinted by permission of Andrews and McMeel, Inc.

The Lives of a Cell, by Lewis Thomas. Copyright 1972, 1973, by the Massachusetts Medical Society. Selections reprinted by permission of Viking Penguin, Inc.

War and Peace, by Leo Tolstoy, translated by Louise and Aylmer Maude. Copyright 1942 by Simon and Schuster, Inc. Selections reprinted by permission of Oxford University Press.

St. Thomas Aquinas, by Gerald Vann. Copyright 1947 by Benziger Brothers, Inc. Selections reprinted by permission of Benziger, Division of Glencoe Publishing Co., Inc.

Candide and Other Writings, by Voltaire, edited by Haskell M. Block. Copyright 1956 by Random House, Inc. Selections reprinted by permission of Random House, Inc.

Caryll Houselander: That Divine Eccentric, by Maisie Ward. Copyright 1962 by Sheed and Ward. Selection reprinted by permission of Andrews and McMeel, Inc.

The Simone Weil Reader, edited by George A. Panichas. Copyright 1977 by David McKay Company, Inc. Selections reprinted by permission of David McKay Company, Inc.

Waiting for God, by Simone Weil, translated by Emma Craufurd. Copyright 1951, renewed by G. P. Putnam's Sons. Selection reprinted by permission of G. P. Putnam's Sons.

The Bridge of San Luis Rey, by Thornton Wilder. Copyright 1927 by Albert and Charles Boni, Inc. Copyright renewed 1955 by Thornton Wilder. Selections reprinted by permission of Harper & Row, Publishers, Inc.

CONTENTS

There Is A Season

JANUARY

IT IS IN JANUARY that new beginnings and new resolutions abound, that the northwest wind chills the body and the soul, that skates scrape the ice in marvelous figures, that aged birds fall for the last time from a friendly branch, that distant stars touch the earth in the clarity of a frozen night, that spring seems too distant to provide glory, that airports rest under the cover of a malicious blizzard, that southern climates draw northern folk like magnets, that teachers despair of the far-distant Easter, that the land goes into its deepest sleep in preparation for summer work. *These have been some of my Januarys—what about yours?*

It is in January that certain questions run through my heart:

   whence anger?
     why so many frozen tears of hatred and indifference?
   whence gifts?
     why so many blessings and graces for our poor spirits?
   whence loneliness?
     why so much anguish and angst throughout history?
   whence remembering?
     why do we travel so often into the land of the past filled with hopes and fears?
   whence hell?
     why that total coldness and darkness of being?

These have been some of my Januarys—what about yours?

IT WAS IN JANUARY that certain lessons and insights came home: that dormancy is as important and as fruitful as high activity; that each day and year is sheer gift; that blizzards are instruments of surprise, disrupting our control of life; that fields in this season are not disposed to winter rains, much like the seasons of the human heart. *These have been some of my Januarys—what about yours?*

A January Poem

STRATIFIED SNOW

The plow-cut banks reveal
chocolate-marbled layers
of frozen slush
re-snowed on,
thawed,
covered again.
And so winter continues
the rhythm
some see as harsh.
Stripping nature
to its brown, black bones,
it bares in teeth-chatter chill
what spring's filigree
and summer's growth
so carefully hide.
Even with shortened
sun time,
weaknesses and faults
of man and God creations
are put forth plainly
and proclaimed
by bold, cold winter,
between its blowing storms
or gentle snowfalls.
It is not the season
for the shallow or shy.
It is a time
when reality
is revealed,
inside
and out.

Barbara J. Holt

Theme:

Anger – Frozen Tears

. . . for anger always needs something to punish.[1] (A. Manzoni)

God's Word: Dt. 9:7–14

Personal Reflection:

1

I was angry with my friend:
I told my wrath, my wrath did end.
I was angry with my foe:
I told it not, my wrath did grow.[2] (Wm. Blake)

God's Word: Eph. 2:3–6

Personal Reflection:

2

Men are not angered by mere misfortune but by misfortune conceived as injury.[3] (C. S. Lewis)

God's Word: Jn. 2:13–22

Personal Reflection:

3

What another man would take as an occasion for anger at me, this sincere young man took as a reason for becoming angry at himself and for loving me more ardently. Long ago you had said and had inserted it into your books, ''Rebuke a wise man, and he will love you.''[4] (Augustine)

God's Word: Lk. 9:51–56

Personal Reflection:

4

They knew that a man so hurt and so perplexed may turn in anger, even on people he loves. They left the men alone to figure and to wonder in the dust.[5] (John Steinbeck)

God's Word: Gen. 4:23–24

Personal Reflection:

5

Kent: Yes, Sir; but anger hath a privilege.
Cornwall: Why art thou angry?
Kent: That such a slave as this should wear a sword,
                Who wears no honesty.[6] (Shakespeare)

God's Word: Mk. 6:17–29.

Personal Reflection:

6

And the little prince broke into a lovely peal of laughter, which irritated me very much. I like my misfortunes to be taken seriously.[7] (Antoine de Saint Exupéry)

God's Word: 1 Cor. 1:10–16

Personal Reflection:

7

Theme:

Gifts – Bowed Packages

Rings and other jewels are not gifts, but apologies for gifts. The only gift is a portion of thyself. Thou must bleed for me. Therefore the poet brings his poem; the shepherd, his lamb; the farmer, corn; the miner, a gem; the sailor, coral and shells; the painter, his picture; the girl, a handkerchief of her own sewing.[8] (Emerson)

God's Word: Rom. 5:1–11

Personal Reflection:

8

The gift is to receive the prophet, to receive the just man, to offer a cup of cold water to a disciple.[9] (Augustine)

God's Word: Gen. 18:1–8

Personal Reflection:

9

God usually does not bestow a favor upon the body without bestowing it first and principally upon the soul.[10] (John of the Cross)

God's Word: Acts 9:1–19

Personal Reflection:

10

Spiritual gifts are worthless in themselves unless they help to build up the community and are inspired by authentic love.[11] (Jon Sobrino)

God's Word: 1 Cor. 12:4–11

Personal Reflection:

11

But yet, Lord, thanks must be given to you, our God, the most excellent and best creator and ruler of the universe, even if you had willed only to bring me to childhood. Even then I existed, had life and feeling, had care for my own well-being, which is a trace of your own most mysterious unity from which I took my being. By my inner sense I guarded the integrity of my outer senses, and I delighted in truth, in these little things and in thoughts about these little things. I did not want to err; I was endowed with a strong memory; I was well instructed in speech; I was refined by friendship. I shunned sadness, dejection, and ignorance. What was there that was not wonderful and praiseworthy in such a living being?

All these things are the gifts of my God: I did not give them to myself.[12] (Augustine)

God's Word: Ps. 136

Personal Reflection:

12

Be a gift and a benediction.[13] (Emerson)

God's Word: 1 Tim. 6:11–16

Personal Reflection:

13

For in spiritual things he has had a great deal of experience in a short time, these being gifts bestowed by God when He wills and as He wills and having nothing to do either with time or with service.[14] (Teresa of Avila)

God's Word: Rom. 11:33–36

Personal Reflection:

14

Theme:

Loneliness – Haunting Blizzards

And it is a comfort to me to know that others, especially such a prophet as this, have experienced that great extremity of loneliness.[15] (Teresa of Avila)

God's Word: Ps. 42–43

Personal Reflection:

15

Nunquam minus solus, quam cum solus.[16] (Never less lonely than when alone). (John Henry Newman)

God's Word: Mt. 4:1–11

Personal Reflection:

_____ **16**

. . . and now who cares? It was so with me almost every evening of my life; one little stairway led me from feast or council, all the bustle and skill and glory of queenship, to my own chamber to be alone with myself—that is, with nothingness. Going to bed and waking in the morning (I woke, most often, too early) were bad times—so many hundreds of evenings and mornings.[17] (C.S. Lewis)

God's Word: 2 Sam. 19:1–8

Personal Reflection:

_____ **17**

He was precise about his Indian relics as he was precise about everything, but I sensed after a while a touch of pathos—the pathos of a man clinging to order in a world where the wind changed the landscape before morning, and not even a dog could help you contain the loneliness of your days.[18] (Loren Eiseley)

God's Word: Job 3:3–26

Personal Reflection:

_____ **18**

Loneliness does not come from having no people about one, but from being unable to communicate the things that seem important to oneself.[19] (C.G. Jung)

God's Word: Jn. 4:1–10

Personal Reflection:

_____ **19**

And always, if he had a little money, a man could get drunk. The hard edges gone, and the warmth. Then there was no loneliness, for a man could people his brain with friends, and he could find his enemies and destroy them. Sitting in a ditch, the earth grew soft under him. Failures dulled and the future was no threat. And hunger did not sulk about, but the world was soft and easy, and man could reach the place he started for. The stars came down wonderfully close and the sky was soft. Death was a friend, and sleep was death's brother.[20] (John Steinbeck)

God's Word: Gal. 5:19–21

Personal Reflection:

20

A person can be lonely even if he is loved by many people, because he is not the "One and Only" to anyone.[21] (Anne Frank)

God's Word: Jn. 8:3–11

Personal Reflection:

21

Theme:

Remembering (Memory) – Quiet Fireside

. . . but he gathered that books were few in Malacandra. 'It is better to remember,' said the sorns.[22] (C. S. Lewis)

God's Word: Gen. 37:5–11

Personal Reflection:

22

. . . and there are persons he cannot choose but remember, who gave a transcendent expansion to his thought, and kindled another life in his bosom.[23] (Emerson)

God's Word: Lk. 2:51–52

Personal Reflection:

23

Those who have fallen may remember the fall, even when they forget the height.[24] (G. K. Chesterton)

God's Word: Gen. 3:1–24

Personal Reflection:

24

God gives us memory so that we may have roses in December.[25] (Sir James Barrie)

God's Word: Mt. 16:1–4

Personal Reflection:

25

Lydia:"Ah! Madam! our memories are independent of our wills. —It is not so easy to forget."[26] (Sheridan)

God's Word: Jer. 31:31–34

Personal Reflection:

26

Within the wine-hall he found the warriors
Fast in slumber, forgetting grief,
Forgetting the woe of the world of men.[27] (Beowulf)

God's Word: Mk. 14:32–42

Personal Reflection:

27

Six years have already passed since my friend went away from me, with his sheep. If I try to describe him here, it is to make sure that I shall not forget him. To forget a friend is sad. Not everyone has had a friend. And if I forget him, I may become like the grown-ups who are no longer interested in anything but figures. . . .[28] (Antoine de Saint Exupéry)

God's Word: Lk. 22:1–6

Personal Reflection:

28

Theme:

Hell – Lifeless Ice

Some say the world will end in fire,
Some say in ice.
From what I've tasted of desire
I hold with those who favor fire.
But if it had to perish twice,
I think I know enough of hate
To say that for destruction ice
Is also great
And would suffice.[29] (Robert Frost)

God's Word: Mt. 23:33–36.

Personal Reflection:

29

We must picture Hell as a state where everyone is perpetually concerned about his own dignity and advancement, where everyone has a grievance, and where everyone lives the deadly serious passions of envy, self-importance, and resentment.[30] (C. S. Lewis)

God's Word: Lk. 16:19–31

Personal Reflection:

30

Mephistophilis: So now Faustus, ask me what thou wilt.
Faustus: First will I question with thee about Hell.
                Tell me, where is the place that men call Hell?
Mephistophilis: Under the heavens.
Faustus: Ay, so are all things else, but whereabouts?
Mephistophilis: Within the bowels of these elements
                Where we are tortur'd and remain forever.
                Hell hath no limits nor is circumscrib'd
                In one self place, but where we are is Hell,
                And where Hell is there must we ever be.
                And to be short, when all the world dissolves
                And every creature shall be purifi'd
                All places shall be Hell that is not Heaven!
Faustus: I think Hell's a fable.
Mephistophilis: Ay, think so still—till experience change thy mind![31] (Christopher Marlowe)

God's Word: Mk. 9:42–50.

Personal Reflection:

31

FEBRUARY

IT IS IN FEBRUARY that ground hogs are always expected but never seen, that small pieces of candy with "I love you" are passed surreptitiously between aisles in the fourth grade classroom, that a president is shot and another greatly honored, that snowplows do the Flying Dutchman in the snow, that the hibernating bear senses the limitation of natural resources, that the ski lift longs for the less weary days of July, that the fruit cellar tells of prudent planning, that teachers go bananas, that the basketball and boy become one after months of adjustments. *These have been some of my Februarys— what about yours?*

> *It is in February that certain questions run through my heart:*
> whence hope?
>   why this resident within the human breast?
> whence love?
>   why that enchanted evening when only the fool would dare say why?
> whence faith?
>   why the blessedness of not seeing and yet believing?
> whence God?
>   why do our finite minds and hearts attempt to embrace the
>   Incomprehensible?
>
> *These have been some of my Februarys—what about yours?*

IT WAS IN FEBRUARY that certain lessons and insights came home: that not all months are equal—some are more gifted than others; that in some way every person is lovable and huggable; that killing, while destroying the victim, annihilates the victimizer; that expertise results from years of assumed discipline; that even time must leap at least once in every five years; that the memory allows us to carry summer's warmth and flowers into the most discontent of winters; that coldness often paralyzes—as in the gas line freeze. *These have been some of my Februarys—what about yours?*

A February Poem

STRIPPED TREE

Alone it stands and silent, a stripped tree,
Robbed of its leaves, its nesting birds all flown.
Round it and through it bitter winds have blown,
Testing its strength by stern adversity.
Serene it stands tonight all sorrow-free,
Silvered with starlight, its branches radiant grown.
Had it been green with boughs I had not known
This rarer beauty now revealed to me.

I am that silent tree upon the hill:
Strip me of all my leaves, even of my song
If stark against the sky I can fulfill
My quest for ultimate Beauty. Not for long
Endures the darkness of earth's bleakest night
Serene the stars break through with silver light.

Ruth Mary Fox

Theme:

Hope – Awakened
          Ground Hog

We judge a man's wisdom by his hope.[32] (Emerson)
God's Word: Rom. 8:18–27.

Personal Reflection:

_____ **1**

And when we had talked together for a great time hope returned to me . . .[33] (C. S. Lewis)
God's Word: Lk. 24:13–35.

Personal Reflection:

_____ **2**

However, Candide had one great advantage over Martin, because he still hoped to see Mademoiselle Cunegonde again, and Martin had nothing to hope for.[34] (Voltaire)
God's Word: Mt. 27:3–10.

Personal Reflection:

_____ **3**

Lady Macbeth: Was the hope drunk,
                Wherein you dress'd yourself?[35] (Shakespeare)

God's Word: Eph. 5:1–20.

Personal Reflection:

_____ **4**

A hopeless life of unfilled desire.[36] (Dante)

God's Word: Mt. 14:3–10

Personal Reflection:

_____ **5**

He thinks if he could teach him that, he'd be
Some good perhaps to someone in the world.
He hates to see a boy the fool of books.
Poor Silas, so concerned for other folks,
And nothing to look backward to with pride,
And nothing to look forward to with hope,
So now and never any different.[37] (Robert Frost)

God's Word: Lk. 13:6–9

Personal Reflection:

_____ **6**

If . . . If . . . and we went on adding dark stanza after dark stanza to this dirge of our distress. But there was always this conditional mood in our souls. There was always that little ray of hope, that door half open on the road to daylight.[38] (Raïssa Maritain)

God's Word: Ruth 2

Personal Reflection:

_____ **7**

Theme:

Love – Joyful Valentine Card

Hence his loves might, if you wished, be all described as cupboard loves: food and warmth, hands that caressed, voices that reassured, were their objects.[39] (C. S. Lewis)

God's Word: 2 Sam. 11:1–27.

Personal Reflection:

_____ **8**

Do not waste time bothering whether you "love" your neighbor; act as if you did. As soon as we do this we find one of the great secrets. When you are behaving as if you loved someone, you will presently come to love him.[40] (C. S. Lewis)

God's Word: Mt. 25:31–46.

Personal Reflection:

_____ **9**

. . . and Boratynskij's correction of Descartes: *amo ergo sum,* is pertinent.[41] (Gerald Vann)

God's Word: 1 Jn. 4:7–11.

Personal Reflection:

_____ **10**

We could almost say He sees because He loves, and therefore loves although He sees.[42] (C. S. Lewis)

God's Word: Is. 43:1–5.

Personal Reflection:

11

One cannot love many at one time; one cannot really have many friends.[43] (John Henry Newman)

God's Word: Rom. 12:9–13.

Personal Reflection:

12

Goneril: Sir, I love you more than word can wield the matter;
        Dearer than eyesight, space, and liberty;
        Beyond what can be valued, rich or rare;
        No less than life, with grace, health, beauty, honour;
        As much as child e'er loved, or father found;
        A love that makes breath poor, and speech unable.
        Beyond all manner of so much I love you.[44] (Shakespeare)

God's Word: Sg: 2:8–3:5.

Personal Reflection:

13

And we are put on earth a little space,
That we may learn to bear the beams of love.[45] (Wm. Blake)

God's Word: Lk. 22:61–62.

Personal Reflection:

14

Theme:

Faith – Darkened Days

The discrepancy between faith and the facts is greater than is generally assumed.[46] (Thornton Wilder)

God's Word: Mt. 14:22–33.

Personal Reflection:

15

You never know how much you really believe anything until its truth or falsehood becomes a matter of life and death to you. . . Only a real risk tests the reality of a belief.[47] (C. S. Lewis)

God's Word: Gen. 22:1–19.

Personal Reflection:

16

Communists are bound together by no secret oath. The tie that binds them across the frontiers of nations, across barriers of language and differences of class and education, in defiance of religion, morality, truth, law, honor, the weaknesses of the body and the irresolutions of the mind, even unto death, is a simple conviction: It is necessary to change the world. Their power, whose nature baffles the rest of the world, because in a large measure the rest of the world has lost that power, is the power to hold convictions and to act on them. It is the same power that moves mountains; it is also an unfailing power to move men. Communists are that part of mankind which has recovered the power to live or die—to bear witness—for its faith. And it is a simple, rational faith that inspires men to live or die for it.[48] (W. Chambers)

God's Word: Mk. 7:1–7.

Personal Reflection:

17

His faith is great; I cannot touch his soul.[49] (Christopher Marlowe)

God's Word: Acts 7:1–60.

Personal Reflection:

18

Our faith comes in moments; our vice is habitual.[50] (Emerson)

God's Word: Gal. 1:6–10.

Personal Reflection:

19

The moral of all this is an old one; that religion is revelation. In other words, it is a vision, and a vision received by faith; but it is a vision of reality. The faith consists in a conviction of its reality. That, for example, is the difference between a vision and day-dream. And that is the difference between religion and mythology.[51] (G. K. Chesterton)

God's Word: Lk. 9:28–36.

Personal Reflection:

20

It is of the essence of faith to let God be God.[52] (Jon Sobrino)

God Word: Dt. 8:1–6.

Personal Reflection:

21

Theme:

God – Silent Snowfall

The transition from the good man to the saint is a sort of revolution; by which one for whom all things illustrate and illuminate God becomes one for whom God illustrates and illuminates all things.[53] (G. K. Chesterton)

God's Word: Jn. 1:35–51.

Personal Reflection:

22

I had approached God, or my idea of God, without love, without awe, even without fear.[54] (C. S. Lewis)

God's Word: Lk. 18:9–14.

Personal Reflection:

23

Anna was not only deeply in love with Mister God; she was proud of him. Anna's pride in Mister God grew and grew to such dimensions that in some idiotic moment I wondered if Mister God ever went pink with pleasure. Whatever feelings people have had about Mister God over the many centuries, I'm sure of one thing—nobody has ever liked Mister God more than Anna.[55] (Fynn)

God's Word: Ps. 150.

Personal Reflection:

24

I enter into the presence of God with all my load of misery and troubles. And he takes me just as I am and makes me to be alone with Him.[56] (Raïssa Maritain)

God's Word: Rom. 7:14–25.

Personal Reflection:

25

God created all things with remarkable ease and brevity, and in them He left some trace of Who He is, not only in giving all things being from nothing, but even by endowing them with innumerable graces and qualities, making them beautiful in a wonderful order and unfailing dependence on one another. All of this He did through His own wisdom, the Word, His only begotten Son by Whom He created them.[57] (John of the Cross)

God's Word: Prov. 8:22–31.

Personal Reflection:

26

. . . my God is not in the least meticulous.[58] (Teresa of Avila)

God's Word: Eph. 3:14–21.

Personal Reflection:

_____ **27**

Insofar as human beings do not let God be God, they themselves cease to be human.[59] (Jon Sobrino)

God's Word: 1 Sam. 19:8–10.

Personal Reflection:

_____ **28**

MARCH

IT IS IN MARCH that Shakespeare tells of betrayal and death, that high winds come out of the universe to test the hearts of man and beast, that ice repents of its frigidity and begins the process of conversion, that the snakes in Ireland have one hell of a time, that small children tied to kites are pulled from the earth (and an adult or two as well), that students fancy a bonfire of books, that ditches plus snow plus a fifth grade boy make Boulder Dam look like peanuts, that sugar maple trees identify with Silas Marner no longer, that the baseball glove is considered for promotion, that winter and spring enter the courts to see who gets custody of time. *These have been some of my Marches—what about yours?*

> *It is in March that certain questions run through my heart:*
> whence death?
> > why did my dog and father and sister have to die?
>
> whence joy?
> > why that jubilant movement when we know that we are gifted and are gifts?
>
> whence freedom?
> > why does God give us such power for good or ill?
>
> whence disposition?
> > why the roller-coaster cycles of history and
> > the human spirit?
>
> whence paradox?
> > why so much grayness when black and white are so comfortable?

These have been some of my Marches—what about yours?

IT WAS IN MARCH that certain lessons and insights came home: that taking time is a fundamental rule of happiness; that the golden rule can be interpreted—"he who has the gold makes the rule"; that Brutus never died—he never really lived; that distaste for genius happens when that genius is offered in the wrong season (Shakespeare to the ill-disposed); that a summer day in March cannot last; that a kite without a tail and a person without roots lack essential stability; that a season and a person should not overstay their welcome. *These have been some of my Marches—what about yours?*

A March Poem

We like March—his shoes are Purple.
He is new and high—
Makes he Mud for Dog and Peddler—
Makes he Forests Dry—
Knows the Adder's Tongue his coming
And begets her spot—
Stands the Sun so close and mighty—
That our Minds are hot.
News is he of all the others—
Bold it were to die
With the Blue Birds buccaneering
On his British sky—

Emily Dickinson

Theme:

Death – Fearful Ides

Nothing that has not died will be resurrected.[60] (C. S. Lewis)
God's Word: 2 Cor. 5:6–10.

Personal Reflection:

_____   **1**

Death is better for every earl
Than life besmirched with the brand of shame.[61] (Beowulf)
God's Word: 2 Mac. 7:1–29.

Personal Reflection:

_____   **2**

The unbearable tragedy is not death but dying in an alien arena—separated from dignity, separated from the warmth of familiar things, separated from the ever-present ministrations of a loving relationship and an outstretched hand.[62] (Norman Cousins)
God's Word: Dt. 32:48–52.

Personal Reflection:

_____   **3**

Death—comes for us all, my lords. Yes, even for Kings he comes, to whom amidst all their Royalty and brute strength he will neither kneel nor make them any reverence nor pleasantly desire them to come forth, but roughly grasp them by the very breast and rattle them until they be stark dead![63] (Robert Bolt)

God's Word: 1 Kg. 2:1–11.

Personal Reflection:

4

Death cannot be bitter to the soul that loves, for in it she finds all the sweetness and delight of love. The thought of death cannot sadden her, for she finds that gladness accompanies this thought. Neither can the thought of death be burdensome and painful to her, for death will put an end to all her sorrows and afflictions and be the beginning of all her bliss. She thinks of death as her friend and bridegroom, and at the thought of it she rejoices as she could over the thought of her betrothal and marriage, and she longs for that day and that hour of her death more than earthly kings yearn for kingdoms and principalities.[64] (John of the Cross)

God's Word: Phil. 1:21–26.

Personal Reflection:

5

Churches and cities, which have diseases like to men,
Must have like death that we have.[65] (John Webster)

God's Word: Tb. 14:12–15.

Personal Reflection:

6

But he brought a lifetime of prayer with him to death's door; and in a little while it entered there with him.[66] (Paul Horgan)

God's Word: Gen. 5:21–24.

Personal Reflection:

7

Theme:

Joy – Soaring Kite

Let me tell it my way. One cannot come into possession of joy and keep secrets.[67] (Jean Montaurier)
God's Word: 1 Jn. 1:1–4.

Personal Reflection:

_____ **8**

In fact, joy is the truth of the happy life.[68] (Augustine)
God's Word: Is. 9:1–2.

Personal Reflection:

_____ **9**

For it was a spiritual joy; my soul knew that here was a soul that would understand and be in harmony with mine.[69] (Teresa of Avila)
God's Word: Jn. 16:22–24.

Personal Reflection:

_____ **10**

Joy silenced me.[70] (C. S. Lewis)

God's Word: Lk. 1:11–22

Personal Reflection:

11

Joy! A kind of pride, a gaiety, an absurd hope, entirely carnal, the carnal form of hope, I think, is what they call joy. Anyway, I felt young, really young, with this companion who was as young as I.[71] (Bernanos)

God's Word: Rev. 19:7.

Personal Reflection:

12

In truth, between my wonder and my joy,
I felt no wish to listen or to speak.[72] (Dante)

God's Word: Ps. 16:8–11.

Personal Reflection:

13

The intelligence can only be led by desire. For there to be desire, there must be pleasure and joy in the work. The intelligence only grows and bears fruit in joy. The joy of learning is as indispensable in study as breathing is in running. Where it is lacking there are no real students, but only poor caricatures of apprentices who, at the end of their apprenticeship, will not even have a trade.[73] (Simone Weil)

God's Word: Phil. 4:4–9.

Personal Reflection:

14

Theme:

Freedom – Northbound Geese

Even in midwinter, a man can choose.[74] (Walter Kerr)

God's Word: Jn. 18:1–11.

Personal Reflection:

15

But at this moment I came upon myself. Previously I had existed, too, but everything had merely happened to me. Now I happened to myself. Now I knew: I am myself now, now I exist. Previously I had been willed to do this and that; now I willed.[75] (C. G. Jung)

God's Word: Lk. 10:29–37.

Personal Reflection:

16

Just so my look gave freedom to her tongue.[76] (Dante)

God's Word: Jn. 11:32–37.

Personal Reflection:

17

When one knows of what man is capable, for better and for worse, one also knows that it is not the human being himself who must be protected, but the possibilities he has within him—in other words, his freedom. I confess, insofar as I am concerned, that I cannot love all humanity except with a vast and somewhat abstract love. But I love a few men, living or dead, with such force and admiration that I am always eager to preserve in others what will someday perhaps make them resemble those I love. Freedom is nothing else but a chance to be better, whereas enslavement is a certainty of the worst.[77] (Camus)

God's Word: Lk. 14:15–24.

Personal Reflection:

18

But nobody noticed when the albatross had disappeared.[78] (C. S. Lewis)

God's Word: Lk. 15:11–32.

Personal Reflection:

19

Those who people the factory do not feel them [simple joys], except in rare and fleeting moments, for they are not free.[79] (Simone Weil)

God's Word: Mt. 21:12–17.

Personal Reflection:

20

And freedom cannot abide in a heart dominated by the appetites—in a slave's heart; it dwells in a liberated heart, which is a son's heart.[80] (John of the Cross)

God's Word: Gal. 4:3–7.

Personal Reflection:

21

Theme:

Disposition – Ambivalent Winds

To the poet, to the philosopher, to the saint, all things are friendly and sacred, all events profitable, all days holy, all men divine.[81] (Emerson)

God's Word: Col. 1:3–14.

Personal Reflection:

22

For one moment I was in the mood in which men burned witches. . .[82] (G. K. Chesterton)

God's Word: 2 Kg. 1:9–11.

Personal Reflection:

23

. . . and as always happens to those in bad humor, it seemed to him that everyone regarded him with aversion and that he was in everybody's way.[83] (Tolstoy)

God's Word: Gen. 4:1–16.

Personal Reflection:

24

No man can learn what he has not preparation for learning, however near to his eye is the object. A chemist may tell his most precious secrets to a carpenter, and he shall be never the wiser—the secrets he would not utter to a chemist for an estate. God screens us evermore from the premature ideas. Our eyes are holden that we cannot see things that stare us in the face, until the hour arrives when the mind is ripened; then we behold them, and the time when we saw them not is like a dream.[84] (Emerson)

God's Word: Mt. 13:4–9.

Personal Reflection:

25

Wisdom and goodness to the vile seem vile.[85] (Shakespeare)

God's Word: Jn. 7:45–52.

Personal Reflection:

26

From experience I knew it is no strange thing that the bread that pleases a healthy appetite is offensive to one that is not healthy, and that light is hateful to sick eyes, but welcome to the well.[86] (Augustine)

God's Word: Mt. 12:38–42.

Personal Reflection:

27

It depends on the mood of the man whether he shall see the sunset or the fine poem.[87] (Emerson)

God's Word: Col. 4:2–6.

Personal Reflection:

28

Theme:

Paradox – Rising,
            Falling Sun

What lies closest is most difficult to grasp; what is nearest is most unclear; what is simplest is most difficult.[88] (L. Boros)

God's Word: Lk. 9:24.

Personal Reflection:

29

How from sweet seed can issue bitterness?[89] (Dante)

God's Word: Gen. 37:12–20.

Personal Reflection:

_____ **30**

The life of prayer is perhaps the most mysterious of all human experience. We come to be at home with a God we cannot see. We discover that it is only by giving ourselves away totally that we truly come to possess ourselves, that we are most free when most surrendered. We begin to realize that light is darkness and darkness light. We become lost in a trackless desert—and then, if we persevere despite our disorientation, we begin to realize that it is only in being lost, in losing ourselves, that we are found. The whole of our life, and not just our prayer life, becomes a paradox, an apparent contradiction concealing and revealing a deeper truth, because we begin to realize that we must live as we pray.[90] (Thomas Green)

God's Word: Mt. 19:27–30.

Personal Reflection:

_____ **31**

APRIL

IT IS IN APRIL that rivers become bloated with power and pride, that an early robin returns, too soon, to open her northern cottage, that heaven's rainbarrels, filled with too many tears, overflow and water the earth, that the vats in the forest collect golden syrup from generous trees, that the sound of bat and ball stimulate the roar of the crowd, that the elderly sigh with another winter behind them, that summer plans turn from myth to partial reality, that the Easter lily tells that all will be well, that blossoms paint the sky in delicate hues, that the early morning sound of well-nourished geese stirs the human spirit to great achievements, that love cannot be hidden though one is silent. *These have been some of my Aprils—what about yours?*

It is in April that certain questions run through my heart:
    whence happiness?
      why such an elusive gnome seen by few and desired by all?
    whence life?
      why the gift of "to be" so freely given to bee and me?
    whence peace?
      why the search for harmony in heart and home?
    whence suffering?
      why this mystery touching every life and age?
    whence riddles?
      why do questions always win over answers?
These have been some of my Aprils—what about yours?

IT WAS IN APRIL that certain lessons and insights came home: that the cause-effect relationship although true is not as simple as April showers bringing May flowers; that death-resurrection is a single piece and remains forever inseparable; that an April fool is March's wise man; that necessity (tax forms) gets things done; that warm environments in their affirmation of nature do great things; that erasers are important instruments of education; that a blossom petal and human flesh have texture. *These have been some of my Aprils—what about yours?*

An April Poem

PUDDLES AND PICNIC PLACES

Mistiness fogs vision
  yet softly caresses my face
    because summer air is gentle at 7 a.m.
In an hour as more feet go by
  and more feet move faster
sodoestheshowerwithdropsracingoneanother
toearthonthebreeze.

The rushing wind
  whooshes water down
  in torrents
  by 9
  and whirls
  the day past
  to 2 p.m.
  when blinding sun
b u r s t s through departing storm clouds
to warm and welcome
early afternoon's features.

By 7 p.m. there's a change of attire,
  a slow-burning fire and
only a brief glint of the day's rain
remaining.

The breeze playfulling tugs
  at paper plates and cups
that are snatched back by hands having fun.
What would it all be,
    reflected sunset asks me,
  if the misty day'd never begun
that way.

Barbara J. Holt

Theme:

Happiness – Warm Showers

For until I am substantially united to him, I can never have perfect rest or true happiness, until, that is, I am so attached to him that there can be no created thing between my God and me.[91] (Julian of Norwich)

God's Word: Rom. 8:31–39.

Personal Reflection:

1

. . . when I am but happy, I ask for no more.[92] (Kierkegaard)

God's Word: Ps. 126.

Personal Reflection:

2

Hedda: I know of no reason why I should be—happy. Perhaps you can give me one?[93]
     (Ibsen)

God's Word: Eph. 1:3–14.

Personal Reflection:

3

Nothing is more difficult to know than the nature of unhappiness; a residue of mystery will always cling to it. For, following the Greek proverb, it is dumb. To seize its exact shadings and causes presupposes an aptitude for inward analysis which is not characteristic of the unhappy. Even if that aptitude existed in this or that individual, unhappiness itself would balk such an activity of thought. Humiliation always has for its effect the creation of forbidden zones where thought may not venture and which are shrouded by silence and illusion. When the unhappy complain, they almost always complain in superficial terms, without voicing the nature of their true discontent; moreover, in cases of profound and permanent unhappiness, a strongly developed sense of shame arrests all lamentation. Thus, every unhappy condition among men ceases the silent zone alluded to, in which each is isolated as though on an island. Those who do escape from the island will not look back. The exceptions turn out almost always to be more apparent than real.[94] (Simone Weil)

God's Word: 1 Sam. 1:9–18.

Personal Reflection:

4

Duchess: Man is most happy, when's own actions
        Be arguments and examples of his virtue.[95] (John Webster)

God's Word: Mt. 5:1–12.

Personal Reflection:

5

But because of his suspicious nature he knew little happiness.[96] (Paul Horgan)

God's Word: 1 Sam. 15:24–31.

Personal Reflection:

6

The Renaissance substituted an anthropocentric humanism for the theocentric humanism of the middle ages; and though this shifting of the centre of life was expected to issue in a new age of happiness and perfection for man, in point of fact it excluded two essential elements of the good life, without which happiness is in fact impossible: creatureliness and creativity.[97] (Gerald Vann)

God's Word: Jb. 38–39.

Personal Reflection:

7
_____

Theme:

Life – Golden Flowers

If we live truly, we shall see truly.[98] (Emerson)

God's Word: Gal. 2:19–21.

Personal Reflection:

8
_____

Life is a series of surprises, and would not be worth taking or keeping if it were not. God delights to isolate us every day, and hide from us the past and the future.[99] (Emerson)

God's Word: Mt. 6:25–37.

Personal Reflection:

9

A dead thing can go with the stream, but only a living thing can go against it.[100] (G. K. Chesterton)

God's Word: 2 Cor. 4:7–12.

Personal Reflection:

10

"Well, darling, I do not think of it that way. Do you know what I think? I think it is better to make life than to remember it."[101] (Paul Horgan)

God's Word: Dt. 30:15–20.

Personal Reflection:

11

If I were required to put into a single sentence my own explanation of the state of our hearts, heads, and nerves, I would do it this way: we are vaguely wretched because we are leading half-lives, half-heartedly, and with only one-half of our minds actively engaged in making contact with the universe about us.[102] (Walter Kerr)

God's Word: Ps. 1.

Personal Reflection:

12

She lived too much in the neat little airless room of her mind.[103] (Sinclair Lewis)

God's Word: Mt. 14:3–12

Personal Reflection:

13

Life went on as usual, but had no consequences, that is to say, sounds did not echo or thoughts develop.[104] (E. M. Forster)

God's Word: Mk. 10:17–22

Personal Reflection:

14

Theme:

Peace – Bird's Song

For us, peace is in a good will.[105] (Augustine)
God's Word: Rom. 12:14–21.

Personal Reflection:

_____ **15**

Nothing can bring you peace but the triumph of principles.[106] (Emerson)
God's Word: Is. 2:2–5.

Personal Reflection:

_____ **16**

Sources of peace: God and trees.[107] (Raïssa Maritain)
God's Word: Ps. 52:8–9.

Personal Reflection:

_____ **17**

I would set out by myself before the family was stirring in the morning and spend whole days in the woods, which required of me only that I be silent, patient and harmless. In return, nature gave me the peace that it gives to anyone who comes to see and hear and not to change.[108] (W. Chambers)

God's Word: Lev. 26:3–7.

Personal Reflection:

18

A man who knows his job, who has had enough to eat, and his horse, too, can always sleep peacefully.[109] (Chekhov)

God's Word: Eph. 6:14–17.

Personal Reflection:

19

And this our life, exempt from public haunt,
Finds tongues in trees, books in the running brooks,
Sermons in stones, and good in everything,
I would not change it.[110] (Shakespeare)

God's Word: Ez. 34:23–31.

Personal Reflection:

20

Believe me, unless we have peace, and strive for peace in our home, we shall not find it in the homes of others.[111] (Teresa of Avila)

God's Word: Jn. 20:19–21.

Personal Reflection:

21

Theme:

Suffering – Sorrowful Moon

Everything that was not suffered to the end and finally concluded, recurred, and the same sorrows were undergone.[112] (H. Hesse)

God's Word: 2 Cor. 12:7–10.

Personal Reflection:

_____ 22

Edgar: When we our betters see bearing our woes,
       We scarcely think our miseries our foes.
       Who alone suffers suffers most i' the mind,
       Leaving free things and happy shows behind.[113] (Shakespeare)

God's Word: Mk. 15:40–41.

Personal Reflection:

_____ 23

Usually the suffering of injustice is needed to bring the vision, just as immunity from suffering may obscure it.[114] (J. C. Murray)

God's Word: Acts 16:16–24.

Personal Reflection:

24

All coming into existence is a suffering.[115] (Kierkegaard)

God's Word: Lk. 1:26–38.

Personal Reflection:

25

. . . for the understanding of human suffering is dependent upon justice, and love is its condition.[116] (Simone Weil)

God's Word: Rom. 9:14–24.

Personal Reflection:

26

Through deep suffering people in our country [Russia] have now achieved a spiritual development of such intensity that the Western system in its present state of spiritual exhaustion does not look attractive.[117] (Solzhenitsyn)

God's Word: Jam. 1:2–12.

Personal Reflection:

27

We find suffering that is not wished, suffering that is accepted, and the suffering of love. If God were incapable of suffering in all those ways, and hence in an absolute sense, then God would also be incapable of loving. If love is the acceptance of another without taking thought for one's own well-being, then it contains within itself the capacity for compassion and the freedom to suffer the otherness of the other. An inability to suffer would contradict the basic Christian assertion that God is love.[118] (Jon Sobrino)

God's Word: 1 Pt. 4:12–19.

Personal Reflection:

28

Theme:

Riddles – Questioning Rain

To myself I became a riddle, and I questioned my soul as to why it was sad and why it afflicted me so grievously, and it could answer me nothing.[119] (Augustine)

God's Word: Ps. 25.

Personal Reflection:

29

. . . Queequeg in his own proper person was a riddle to unfold; a wondrous work in one volume; but whose mysteries not even himself could read, though his own live heart beat against them.[120] (Melville)

God's Word: Ps. 39.

Personal Reflection:

30

MAY

IT IS IN MAY that billions of seeds journey into the darkness of the soil, that teachers and students begin their farewells, that parks are peopled, that trees cannot contain their joy and burst into verdant song, that the family dog is not seen for weeks, that mud and boy lose each other by merging, that tents become castles in the backyard, that mosquitoes break jail by the millions and in hordes vandalize every vein in sight, that blue books are filled with truths and stories, that the garage, now empty of wood, awaits an autumn meal, that despair attacks the heart of a rejected doctoral dissertation, that the crack of a gun follows the "On your mark, . . .", that the fields welcome back the housed-in farmer. *These have been some of my Mays—what about yours?*

It is in May that certain questions run through my heart:

whence work?
> why the sweat of the brow and the seeming futility of it all?

whence silence?
> why the stillness of dawn and dusk?

whence beauty?
> why are we captured by a sunset and the human countenance?

whence seeing?
> how can galaxies be gathered into the mind through such a fine instrument as the eye?

whence trust?
> why can people time and again extend their arms despite hurt and pain?

These have been some of my Mays—what about yours?

IT WAS IN MAY that certain lessons and insights came home: that school bells ring two ways: a calling to and sending forth; that the loneliness of the long distant runner is real; that one waits to plant seeds until after Jack Frost has left the country; that every season and friendship has its romantic period; that a golf course is a microcosm of life; that fears and tears are but the same reality; that lilies of the valley make a fine mother's day gift; that the bumblebee, despite its size, is to be carefully respected. *These have been some of my Mays—what about yours?*

A May Poem

SPRING

Nothing is so beautiful as spring—
When weeds, in wheels, shoot long and lovely and lush;
Thrush's eggs look little low heavens, and thrush
Through the echoing timber does so rinse and wring
The ear, it strikes like lightnings to hear him sing;
The glassy peartree leaves and blooms, they brush
The descending blue; that blue is all in a rush
With richness; the racing lambs too have fair their fling.

What is all this juice and all this joy?
A strain of the earth's sweet being in the beginning
In Eden garden. —Have, get, before it cloy,
Before it cloud, Christ, lord, and sour with sinning,
Innocent mind and Mayday in girl and boy,
Most, O maid's child, thy choice and worthy the winning.

Gerard Manley Hopkins

Theme:

Work – Spring Plowing

I said not long before that work and weakness are comforters. But sweat is the kindest creature of the three—far better than philosophy, as a cure for ill thoughts.[121] (C. S. Lewis)

God's Word: Mt. 20:1–6.

Personal Reflection:

_____ **1**

However, I really think it will add to my power of working, and the length of my life. I never wrote more than when I played the fiddle. I always sleep better after music.[122] (John Henry Newman)

God's Word: 1 Cor. 3:5–9.

Personal Reflection:

_____ **2**

"I have only twenty acres," replied the Turk. "I cultivate them with my children; and work keeps at bay three great evils: boredom, vice and need."[123] (Voltaire)

God's Word: 2 Th. 3:6–12.

Personal Reflection:

_____ **3**

"Stigmergy" is a new word, invented recently by Grasse to explain the nest-building behavior of termites, perhaps generalizable to other complex activities of social animals. The word is made of Greek roots meaning "to incite to work," and Grasse's intention was to indicate that it is the product of work itself that provides both the stimulus and instructions for further work.[124] (Lewis Thomas)

God's Word: Lk. 5:4–7.

Personal Reflection:

4

He works his work, I mine.[125] (Tennyson)

God's Word: Ps. 104.

Personal Reflection:

5

Many of these fears were staved off by work. Although religion declined, the significance of work was that it could still mobilize emotional energies into creative challenges. One could eliminate death from consciousness by minimizing it through work.[126] (Daniel Bell)

God's Word: Ex. 1:11–14.

Personal Reflection:

6

Man's work is an extension of himself. It is a revelation of his inner life, both to others and to himself.[127] (Richard Lynch)

God's Word: Ecc. 2:4–11.

Personal Reflection:

7

Theme:

Silence – Flowing Sap

Every secret is told, every crime is punished, every virtue rewarded, every wrong redressed, in silence and certainty.[128] (Emerson)

God's Word: Jam. 3:1–13.

Personal Reflection:

8

Inner silence is for our race a difficult achievement.[129] (C. S. Lewis)

God's Word: Is. 42:14.

Personal Reflection:

9

To know silence perfectly is to know music.[130] (Carl Sandburg)

God's Word: Ps. 46:10.

Personal Reflection:

10

The whole space is filled, even though sounds can be heard, with a dense silence which is not an absence of sound but is a positive object of sensation; it is the secret world, the world of Love who holds us in his arms from the beginning.[131] (Simone Weil)

God's Word: Gal. 1:17–18.

Personal Reflection:

11

Silent music,
In that nocturnal tranquillity and silence and in that knowledge of the divine light the soul becomes aware of Wisdom's wonderful harmony and sequence in the variety of His creatures and works. Each of them is endowed with a certain likeness of God and in its own way gives voice to what God is in it. So creatures will be for the soul a harmonious symphony of sublime music surpassing all concerts and melodies of the world.[132] (John of the Cross)

God's World: Ecc. 3:7.

Personal Reflection:

12

Do you suppose that, because we cannot hear Him, He is silent?[133] (Teresa of Avila)

God's Word: Ps. 44:23–26.

Personal Reflection:

13

There exists, of course, also a "negative silence", a dumb rebelliousness, an unfathomable hostility, a dull lack of interest.[134] (L. Boros)

God's Word: Est. 4:12–14.

Personal Reflection:

14

Theme:

Beauty – Receptive Soil

The ancients called beauty the flowering of virtue.[135] (Emerson)
God's Word: Is. 42:1–4

Personal Reflection:

15

The reader may smile at this as the far-off echo of a precocious calf love, but he will be wrong. There are beauties so unambiguous that they need no lens of that kind to reveal them; they are visible even to the careless and objective eyes of a child.[136] (C. S. Lewis)

God's Word: Ps. 45:10–17.

Personal Reflection:

16

She made beauty all round her.[137] (C. S. Lewis)
God's Word: Gen. 29:15–19.

Personal Reflection:

17

Scientists seldom understand, as artists understand, that one branch of the beautiful is the ugly.[138] (G. K. Chesterton)

God's Word: Lk. 8:43–56.

Personal Reflection:

18

_____

"You [a rose] are beautiful, but you are empty," he [the little prince] went on. "One could not die for you."[139] (Antoine de Saint Exupéry)

God's Word: Hos. 1:2–9.

Personal Reflection:

19

_____

Though we travel the world over to find the beautiful, we must carry it with us, or we find it not.[140] (Emerson)

God's Word: Est. 2:16–17.

Personal Reflection:

20

_____

Behind all these things is the fact that beauty and terror are very real things and related to a real spiritual world; and to touch them at all, even in doubt or fancy, is to stir the deep things in the soul.[141] (G. K. Chesterton)

God's Word: Rev. 21:1–8.

Personal Reflection:

21

_____

Theme:

Seeing – Creative Glance

As I am, so I see.[142] (Emerson)
God's Word: Rev. 1:9–20.

Personal Reflection:

_____ **22**

For what you see and hear depends a good deal on where you are standing; it also depends on what sort of person you are.[143] (C. S. Lewis)
God's Word: 2 Cor. 12:1–6.

Personal Reflection:

_____ **23**

The major quoted the axiom of the Indian fighter—"When you see Apache sign, be careful; and when you see *no* sign, be *more* careful."[144] (Paul Horgan)
God's Word: Lk. 11:29–32.

Personal Reflection:

_____ **24**

There are various ways of being seen. The seeing eye does not merely reflect what it sees, it also acts upon it. Seeing is a creative activity. Seeing influences what it sees.[145] (Romano Guardini)

God's Word: Mk. 2:13–14.

Personal Reflection:

25

This way of looking is first of all attentive. The soul empties itself of all its own contents in order to receive into itself the being it is looking at, just as he is, in all his truth.[146] (Simone Weil)

God's Word: 1 Pt. 1:8–9.

Personal Reflection:

26

. . . it should be known that God's gaze produces four goods in the soul: it cleanses, endows with grace, enriches, and illumines, like the sun that dries and provides warmth and beauty and splendor when it pours down its rays.[147] (John of the Cross)

God's Word: Lk. 19:1–10.

Personal Reflection:

27

We must try to understand the essence of what is presented, and the way in which it is done. This means that seeing must become understanding, as happens in the courtesy of personal encounter, and the receptiveness of listening. We must get rid of the harmful kind of subjectivity composed of impatience, curiosity and ready-made ideas.[148] (L. Boros)

God's Word: Mk. 4:10–12.

Personal Reflection:

28

Theme:

Trust – Sprouting Seeds

I will so trust that what is deep is holy, that I will do strongly before the sun and moon whatever inly rejoices me and the heart appoints.[149] (Emerson)

God's Word: Ps. 37:3–7.

Personal Reflection:

29

Horses and dogs invariably trusted him. He knew their natures for what they were, and while working to make them better through training, he never impatiently required of them more than they could perform. In time he came to apply this gift to dealing with people.[150] (Paul Horgan)

God's Word: Col. 3:12–14.

Personal Reflection:

30

"Be it done unto me according to thy word" surrenders yourself and all that is dear to you to God, and the trust which it implies does not mean trusting God to look after you and yours, to keep you and them in health and prosperity and honor. It means much more, it means trusting that whatever God does with you and with yours is the act of an infinitely loving Father.[151] (Caryll Houselander)

God's Word: Mt. 26:38–43.

Personal Reflection:

31

JUNE

IT IS IN JUNE that children are let loose from school, that the grain of wheat experiences the miracle of death-life, that the sun rises early and stays up late, that trees burst into life attempting to outdo the peacock, that autumn-conceived children emerge into the light of day, that degrees are awarded after years of study and research, that bugs and mosquitoes claim temporary command of the universe, that thousands of green shades decorate the landscape, that leisure is experienced in chunks, that avian engineers construct their sturdy nests. *These have been some of my Junes—what about yours?*

It is in June that certain questions run through my heart:
>whence friendship?
>>why is this delicate and precious gift so freely given?
>
>whence vision?
>>why do some see such large patterns and intricate meanings?
>
>whence thinking?
>>why the constant pondering and searching for truth?
>
>whence health?
>>why are some healthy while others suffer such pain?
>
>whence meaning?
>>why the incessant tension between the mind and the heart?

These have been some of my Junes—what about yours?

IT WAS IN JUNE that certain lessons and insights came home: that August harvests are only possible if June is well tended to; that the longest day has its dark side, the longest night; that education means gaining perspective, seeing things in their interrelatedness; that quiet evening walks are essential to health; that there is inner music (dancing bells) that tells of profound truths. *These have been some of my Junes—what about yours?*

A June Poem

WE WALK IN MIRACLES

We walk in miracles as children scuff
through daisy fields, their dresses appliqued
with shifting tide of blossom, welkin-stuff,
the Father's white creative laughter made.

Common as spring, as bread, as sleep, as salt,
the daisies grow. Our Father made them reel
against us like the morning stars that vault
the greater home His Love will yet reveal.

The petals push against the ankles, knees,
the thigh, the hands; gold pollen sifts within
the pores to rivulets of veins, to seas
of subtle life behind unsubtle skin.

O deeper and deeper than daisy fields, we drown
in miracles, in God, our Seed, our Crown.

Sister Maura, S.S.N.D.

Theme:

Friendship – Dancing Bells

There are two elements that go to the composition of friendship, each so sovereign that I can detect no superiority in either, no reason why either should be first named. One is truth. A friend is a person with whom I may be sincere . . . The other element of friendship is tenderness.[152] (Emerson)

God's Word: Jn. 21:15–19.

Personal Reflection:

_____ **1**

One cannot love many at one time; one cannot really have many friends.[153] (John Henry Newman)
God's Word: Sir. 6:5–17.

Personal Reflection:

_____ **2**

Friendship is the one legitimate exception to the duty of only loving universally.[154] (Simone Weil)
God's Word: Sg. 1:1–4.

Personal Reflection:

_____ **3**

Hence while friendship has been by far the chief source of my happiness, acquaintance or general society has always meant little to me, and I cannot quite understand why a man should wish to know more people than he can make real friends of.[155] (C. S. Lewis)

God's Word: Lk. 12:4–7.

Personal Reflection:

4

Like all solitary persons he had invested friendship with a divine glamour; he imagined that the people he passed on the street, laughing together and embracing when they parted, the people who dined together with so many smiles,—you will scarcely believe me, but he imagined that they were extracting from all that congeniality great store of satisfaction.[156] (Thornton Wilder)

God's Word: Prov. 14:20.

Personal Reflection:

5

The essence of friendship is entireness, a total magnanimity and trust.[157] (Emerson)

God's Word: Jn. 15:13–17.

Personal Reflection:

6

Friendship is almost always the union of a part of one mind with a part of another; people are friends in spots.[158] (George Santayana)

God's Word: Mk. 8:27–33.

Personal Reflection:

7

Theme:

Perspective (Vision) – Lofty
                        Hawk

The difference between landscape and landscape is small, but there is great difference in the beholders.[159] (Emerson)

God's Word: Ps. 145.

Personal Reflection:

_____ **8**

If we want to know the answer to the riddle of life and of the universe, if we want to achieve wisdom, if we want to be fully alive, we must discover a view of reality as a whole in which the answers to individual problems will find their functional place in the organic unity of the whole.[160] (Gerald Vann)

God's Word: Prov. 3:1–35.

Personal Reflection:

_____ **9**

For what you see and hear depends a good deal on where you are standing; it also depends on what sort of person you are.[161] (C. S. Lewis)

God's Word: Ex. 3:1–6.

Personal Reflection:

_____ **10**

We all tend to judge events from the vantage point of this handful of earth beneath our feet. This is a great illusion. We must take our view from the heights and courageously embrace the whole.[162] (John XXIII)

God's Word: Wis. 9:1–12.

Personal Reflection:

11

Marvel: It is harder for you. You had a vision of what might have been. Few of us shared it. We live from day to day.[163] (Don Taylor)

God's Word: Rev. 12:1–17.

Personal Reflection:

12

If, however, we transport our hearts beyond ourselves, beyond the universe, beyond space and time to where our Father dwells, and if from there we behold this mechanism, it appears quite different.[164] (Simone Weil)

God's Word: Jn. 17:24–26.

Personal Reflection:

13

Ulrich was a humble man (which sometimes made lesser people take him for less than he was), well aware of his own limitations, and not at all troubled by them. But his experience of life was great, his reading of men acute, though often he acted directly against what his intelligence told him about them. For his humanity was greater than anything else. And he had the rare faculty of seeing most things from a viewpoint outside of himself.[165] (W. Chambers)

God's Word: 2 Sam. 7:1–17.

Personal Reflection:

14

Theme:

Thinking (thought) – Evening
Walks

What immunity can the world offer a man against his thoughts.[166] (W. Chambers)
God's Word: Ps. 32.

Personal Reflection:

15

But real action is in silent moments. The epochs of our life are not in the visible facts of our choice of a calling, our marriage, our acquisition of an office, and the like, but in a silent thought by the wayside as we walk.[167] (Emerson)
God's Word: Mk. 1:35–39.

Personal Reflection:

16

The human mind is generally far more eager to praise and dispraise than to describe and define.[168]
(C. S. Lewis)
God's Word: Prov. 9:7–12.

Personal Reflection:

17

His colleagues there were embarrassed by his outburst; their defense was that Healy was a warm-hearted man who never thought before he spoke—an unfortunate quality in the editor of a magazine.[169] (Meriol Trevor)

God's Word: Mt. 16:21–23.

Personal Reflection:

18

. . . thy thoughts have created a creature in thee.[170] (Melville)

God's Word: Prov. 17:11.

Personal Reflection:

19

It is remarkable that persons who speculate the most boldly often conform with the most perfect quietude to the external regulations of society. The thought suffices them, without investing itself in the flesh and blood of action.[171] (Hawthorne)

God's Word: Lk. 6:6–11.

Personal Reflection:

20

Hedda: One is not always mistress of one's thoughts.[172] (Ibsen)

God's Word: Wis. 6:1–12.

Personal Reflection:

21

Theme:

Health – Prolific Asparagus

The first health is wealth.[173] (Emerson)

God's Word: Mk. 2:1–12.

Personal Reflection:

22

In the evaluation of selfhood the primary distinction is not the one that divides the sick from the well, but that which separates the developed from the undeveloped. The more complex the self, the more refined its awareness of itself, the more imminent the threat of mental disorder.[174] (Louis Dupré)

God's Word: Jn. 15:1–6

Personal Reflection:

23

They [utilitarians] became first introspective and then introverted; cut off from their fellows as they were, they became secretive and sometimes neurotic. It should surprise no one that vast areas of contemporary art employ a private language, insist upon subjectivity, deliberately refuse to communicate. The man to whom no one speaks is the man most likely to fall sick.[175] (Walter Kerr)

God's Word: Mt. 12:33–37

Personal Reflection:

24

Lear: Infirmity doth still neglect all office
      Whereto our health is bound; we are not ourselves
      When nature, being oppress'd, commands the mind
      To suffer with the body.[176] (Shakespeare)

God's Word: 1 Th. 2:17–20.

Personal Reflection:

25

Nevertheless, it is not just food, medicine and other material which are shared. In some way, they are also the vehicle for human interchange. In sharing my loaf with another I may meet not only his hunger for food but also his hunger for a brother. Health is about sharing, sharing what we have with one another, sharing ourselves with one another. Health is about our relationship to material things, and our relationship to one another. We make health possible for one another.[177] (Michael Wilson)

God's Word: Jn. 6:1–15.

Personal Reflection:

26

Can any person or institution or nation stay healthy without turning outward toward an increasingly public act?[178] (William Lynch)

God's Word: Mt. 28:16–20.

Personal Reflection:

27

The most prevalent—and, for all we know, most serious—health problem of our time is stress. The war against microbes has been largely won, but the struggle for equanimity is being lost. It is not just the congestion outside us—a congestion of people and ideas and issues—but our inner congestion that is hurting us. Our experiences come at us in such profusion and from so many different directions that they are never really sorted out, much less absorbed. The result is clutter and confusion. We gorge the senses and starve the sensitivities.[179] (Norman Cousins)

God's Word: 2 Cor. 8:9.

Personal Reflection:

28

Theme:

Meaning – Riverside Quiet

One of the first characteristics of a mood is that it robs us of all sense of meaning. Relatedness is necessary if we are to have a sense of meaning and fulfillment.[180] (Robert Johnson)

God's Word: Wis. 7:15–21.

Personal Reflection:

29

Because they never went deep enough, they found only *themselves* and in that meeting they began to worry about their lives, their future, what they would leave behind for others to remember. In short, they saw only their mortality and were frightened at the brevity and seeming futility of living, then passing on, in time forgotten by everyone.[181] (Murray Bodo)

God's Word: Jn. 12:37–43.

Personal Reflection:

30

JULY

IT IS IN JULY that the corn is knee high, right to the eye—that swimming holes are revisited by young and old, that a liberty bell is cracked for freedom, that air conditioners do their thing, that all stars begin to shine, that a cold rain is welcomed like a victorious general, that gardens are invited in for dinner, that snow joins the extinct species, that wadis lose their sense of identity, that the sun reaches a midlife crisis. *These have been some of my Julys—what about yours?*

It is in July that certain questions run through my heart:

    whence desire?
      why the longing and yearnings of the human spirit?
    whence time?
      why this transitoriness amid the hunger for the permanent and stable?
    whence poetry?
      why this magnificent instrument of sanity and joy?
    whence prayer?
      why this desire for dialogue with Love when presence would seem to suffice?
    whence heaven?
      why this homeless home for all who experience love?

These have been some of my Julys—what about yours?

IT WAS IN JULY that certain lessons and insights came home: that freedom is acquired only through the pain of bruises and scars; that sanity is fostered through keeping one's hands close to the soil; that inner time must be carefully respected if growth is to follow; that prayer is the gateway to peace; that heaven is being with; that desires carefully tended motivate the development of unique gifts. *These have been some of my Julys—what about yours?*

A July Poem

THE ETERNAL FLIGHT PATTERN

It is hard
      to sit with hands in lap
   when the fledgling fowl
      is learning to fly.
Oh, to be able
   to protect the untested wings
so that feathers
      would never fathom
         a ruffle or bend—
To gently lift
      the gray-soft, warm body
   from nest to worm
so that it would never know
   the harsh reality between—
Oh, to always allow
      a bird . . . . . to fly.

Barbara J. Holt

Theme:

Desire – Haunting
            Independence

Not all that is desired is desirable, and in being moved by my immediate desire I may be balking myself of that ultimate satisfaction which is the real object of all effort. If that is so, then to 'do as I like' may well be no freedom at all.[182] (C. H. Dodd)

God's Word: Col. 3:5–11.

Personal Reflection:

1

Do ye desire a more exalted place—
For wider view,—or state more intimate?[183] (Dante)

God's Word: Mk. 10:35–40.

Personal Reflection:

2

A man is more, much more, than bone and blood and meat. Blood and meat we treat alike when we fight in battle, and we give our orders to them and every man is as useful or not as his neighbor. But when he is hurt or dying or recovering, or longing for whatever it is he longs for, then—then there is something inside him that shows, in ways you cannot put your finger on, and it is the most true thing about him, and the most important.[184] (Paul Horgan)

God's Word: 1 Sam. 17:40–58.

Personal Reflection:

3

One longing is often enough to destroy a man's peace of mind; think, then, of two each conflicting with the other.[185] (A. Manzoni)

God's Word: Jm. 1:13–18.

Personal Reflection:

4

It troubled me with what I can only describe as the Idea of Autumn. It sounds fantastic to say that one can be enamored of a season, but that is something like what happened; and, as before, the experience was one of intense desire. And one went back to the book, not to gratify the desire . . . but to reawake it.[186] (C. S. Lewis)

God's Word: Lk. 12:22–32.

Personal Reflection:

5

This yearning is a spiritual motion,
And rests not till it gains the thing it loves.[187] (Dante)

God's Word: Ps. 123.

Personal Reflection:

6

I believe that it's spring within me, I feel that spring is awakening, I feel it in my whole body and soul. It is an effort to behave normally, I feel utterly confused, don't know what to read, what to write, what to do, I only know that I am longing. . . ![188] (Anne Frank)

God's Word: Lk. 2:36–38.

Personal Reflection:

7

Theme:

Time – Gentle Waiting

Time does not take time off, nor does it turn without purpose through our senses; it works wondrous effects in our minds.[189] (Augustine)

God's Word: Ecc. 3:1–6.

Personal Reflection:

8

The fox gazed at the little prince, for a long time,
''Please—tame me!'' he said.
''I want to, very much,'' the little prince replied. ''But I have not much time. I have friends to discover, and a great many things to undersand.''
''One only understands the things one tames,'' said the fox. ''Men have no more time to understand anything. They buy things all ready made at the shops. But there is no shop anywhere where one can buy friendship, and so men have no friends any more. If you want a friend, tame me. . . .''[190] (Antoine de Saint Exupéry)

God's Word: Jn. 16:16–19.

Personal Reflection:

9

But man postpones or remembers; he does not live in the present, but with reverted eye laments the past, or, heedless of the riches that surround him, stands on tiptoe to foresee the future.[191] (Emerson)

God's Word: Rom. 13:11–14.

Personal Reflection:

10

For the present is the point at which time touches eternity.[192] (C. S. Lewis)

God's Word: Ps. 28.

Personal Reflection:

11

I found, as always, that the ripest are kindest to the raw and the most studious have most time to spare.[193] (C. S. Lewis)

God's Word: Jn. 3:1–21.

Personal Reflection:

12

Great acts take time.[194] (John Henry Newman)

God's Word: Mk. 15:33–39.

Personal Reflection:

13

Time that is lost
Displeases him the most who knows its worth.[195] (Dante)

God's Word: 1 Th. 5:1–3.

Personal Reflection:

Theme:

Poetry – Verbal Melody

It is an odd jealousy, but the poet finds himself not near enough to his object.[196] (Emerson)

God's Word: Ps. 29.

Personal Reflection:

Poetry then is our mysticism; and so far as any two characters of mind tend to penetrate below the surface of things, and to draw men away from the material to the invisible world, so far they may certainly be said to answer the same end; and that to a religious one.[197] (John Henry Newman)

God's Word: Jb. 37.

Personal Reflection:

                                                                                    16

Only theology and poetry can speak of God. Knowledge, inspiration and experience.[198] (Raïssa Maritain)

God's Word: Ph. 2:6–11.

Personal Reflection:

                                                                                    17

And poetry without philosophy has only inspiration, or, in vulgar language, only wind.[199] (G. K. Chesterton)

God's Word: Sir. 19:4–12.

Personal Reflection:

                                                                                    18

Saints have no moderation,
nor do poets,
just exuberance.[200] (Anne Sexton)

God's Word: 1 Cor. 13:1–13.

Personal Reflection:

                                                                                    19

The Incarnation, for instance, "far from denying what we already know of reality, writes the comment which makes the crabbed test plain: or rather, proves itself to be the text on which Nature was only the commentary. In science we have been reading only the notes to a poem; in Christianity we find the poem itself."[201] (C. S. Lewis)

God's Word: Jn. 1:1–18.

Personal Reflection:

20

For one can be a poet only when the word of the mouth breaks forth from the center of the heart. The poet says that which he bears within himself. He expresses himself in truth.[202] (Karl Rahner)

God's Word: Ps. 147.

Personal Reflection:

21

Theme:

Prayer – Summer Intimacy

Prayer is the contemplation of the facts of life from the highest point of view.[203] (Emerson)
God's Word: Ps. 66.

Personal Reflection:

22

In prayer I can enter into contact with the God who created me and all things out of love. In prayer I can find a new sense of belonging since it is there that I am most related.[204] (Henri Nouwen)
God's Word: Mt. 6:5–6.

Personal Reflection:

23

He knew that without prayer true love was impossible, and he learned from living that without love prayer became self-centered and barren.[205] (Murray Bodo)

God's Word: 2 Th. 1:3–11.

Personal Reflection:

24

The key to a Christian conception of studies is the realization that prayer consists of attention. It is the orientation of all the attention of which the soul is capable toward God. The quality of the attention counts for much in the quality of prayer. Warmth of heart cannot make up for it.[206] (Simone Weil)

God's Word: Ecc. 5:1–5.

Personal Reflection:

25

For, although we are always in the presence of God, it seems to me that those who practise prayer are specially so, because they can see all the time that He is looking at them; whereas others may be in God's presence for several days without ever remembering that He can see them.[207] (Teresa of Avila)

God's Word: Jer. 1:4–12.

Personal Reflection:

26

. . . Jesus prayed a certain way because he has a specific conception and personal experience of God. "Prayer" and "God" are correlatives. Whatever problem we find in connection with prayer is simply a reflection of the problem connected with the reality of God.[208] (Jon Sobrino)

God's Word: Mt. 6:7–15.

Personal Reflection:

27

Often enough we think that the dialogue with God should take place in some serene harbor, where the backwash of this world, which we expect to cease in our lives or in our souls in order that we may draw near to him, is not felt. In acting in this way, however, we are in danger of placing under the sign of unreality a relationship which should take its point of departure from what we are and the problems that are ours. So that the Lord may cure us, it is essential for us to come to him with our anguish and our questions.[209] (François Roustang)

God's Word: Ps. 139.

Personal Reflection:

28

Theme:

Heaven – Overflowing Cup

And in this my understanding was lifted up into heaven, where I saw our Lord God as a lord in his own house, who has called all his friends to a splendid feast. Then I did not see him seated anywhere in his own house; but I saw him reign in his house as a king and fill it all full of joy and mirth, gladdening and consoling his dear friends with himself, very familiarly and courteously, with wonderful melody in endless love in his own fair blissful countenance, which glorious countenance fills all heaven full of the joy and bliss of the divinity.[210] (Julian of Norwich).

God's Word: 2 Cor. 5:1–6.

Personal Reflection:

29

To be able to surrender oneself and become "poor" is, in biblical theology, to be with God, to find one's hidden nature in God; in short, it is heaven."[211] (Johannes Metz)

God's Words: Rev. 5:6–12.

Personal Reflection:

30

In heaven she will probably sit between the Heloises and the Cleopatras.[212] (Thomas Hardy)

God's Word: Is. 4:2–6.

Personal Reflection:

31

AUGUST

IT IS IN AUGUST that the butterflies descend-ascend from every crack in the earth and in the heavens, that cabbage toils its way toward the sauerkraut vat, that school bells sound from beyond the hill, that dog days and cat nights cause terror in the human heart, that a scent of autumn creeps into the dusk of day, that geese in northern lands stir toward the south, that daylight loses a moment here, a moment there, that the fields grow rich with harvest, that footballs invade the airways of disturbed birds, that hints of death can no longer be concealed, that hopes are fulfilled or forever laid to rest. *These have been some of my Augusts—what about yours?*

It is in August that certain questions run through my heart:

    whence virtue?
      why this striving after good amid so much chaos and disorder?
    whence wisdom?
      why this deep gift of discerning what is or is not of life?
    whence truth?
      why delve into the fullness of reality regardless of the cost?
    whence person?
      why this complex mystery of body-soul, necessity-possibility, finiteness-infinity?
    whence creativity?
      why use time and energy to make new?

These have been some of my Augusts—what about yours?

IT WAS IN AUGUST that certain lessons and insights came home: that endurance and discipline are essential to growth; that God loves surprises (how else explain butterflies?); that each day provides unique opportunity for giving or taking life; that people tend to get lost in their work and misplace values; that ''making hay while the sun shines'' is a wise adage; that transitions require both evaluation of the past and planning for the future; that dreams are for real; that harvest time is a unique time for community. *These have been some of my Augusts—what about yours?*

An August Poem

Flower in the crannied wall,
I pluck you out of the crannies;
I hold you here, root and all, in my hand,
Little flower—but if I could understand
What you are, root and all, and all in all,
I should know what God and man is.

Alfred, Lord Tennyson

Theme:

Virtue – Benevolent Generator

The ancients called beauty the flowering of virtue.[213] (Emerson)
God's Word: 1 Pt. 2:1–3.

Personal Reflection:

_____ **1**

To be greatly and effectively wicked a man needs some virtue.[214] (C. S. Lewis)
God's Word: Lk. 12:1–3.

Personal Reflection:

_____ **2**

Do not think, even though it may seem so to you, that anyone has acquired a virtue when he
has not tested it by its corresponding vice.[215] (Teresa of Avila)
God's Word: Wis. 2:16–20.

Personal Reflection:

_____ **3**

Of all the different pleasures, they seek mostly those of the mind, and prize them most highly, because most of them arise from the practice of the virtues and the consciousness of a good life.[216] (Thomas More)

God's Word: Sir. 12:1–7.

Personal Reflection:

4

Yesterday I had a good morning. Once again when I recollect myself, I again find the same simple demands of God: gentleness, humility, charity, interior simplicity; nothing else is asked of me. And suddenly I saw clearly why these virtues are demanded, because through them the soul becomes habitable for God and for one's neighbor in an intimate and permanent way. They make a pleasant cell of it. Hardness and pride repel, complexity disquiets. But humility and gentleness welcome, and simplicity reassures. These ''passive'' virtues have an eminently social character.[217] (Raïssa Maritain)

God's Word: Mi. 6:8.

Personal Reflection:

5

An act of virtue produces in a man mildness, peace, comfort, light, purity, and strength, just as inordinate appetite brings about torment, fatigue, weariness, blindness, and weakness.[218] (John of the Cross)

God's Word: Rom. 6:5–7.

Personal Reflection:

6

Nothing is more unpleasant than a virtuous person with a mean mind.[219] (Walter Bagehot)

God's Word: Phm. 1:8–21.

Personal Reflection:

7

Theme:

Wisdom – Prudent Owl

You are wise,
And understand what I have left unsaid.[220] (Dante)

God's Word: Mk. 4:30–32.

Personal Reflection:

8

It [wisdom] is the ability to respond, as a whole man and with some serenity, to the fresh challenge of the previously unknown.[221] (Walter Kerr)

God's Word: Lk. 5:27–28.

Personal Reflection:

9

And that is ever the difference between the wise and unwise: the latter wonders at what is unusual, the wise man wonders at the usual. Shall not the heart which has received so much, trust the Power by which it lives? May it not quit other leadings, and listen to the Soul that has guided it gently and taught it so much, secure that the future will be worthy of the past?[222] (Emerson)

God's Word: Sir. 51:13–38.

Personal Reflection:

10

Persuasive eloquence dates and loses warmth as time blows through it; the thoughts of a wise man only grow as the years pass, like trees.[223] (Meriol Trevor)

God's Word: Sir. 1:1–10.

Personal Reflection:

                                                                                11
_____

True wisdom comes from the overcoming of suffering and sin. All true wisdom is therefore touched with sadness.[224] (W. Chambers)

God's Word: 1 Kg. 8:22–40.

Personal Reflection:

                                                                                12
_____

''Then you shall judge yourself,'' the king answered. ''That is the most difficult thing of all. It is much more difficult to judge oneself than to judge others. If you succeed in judging yourself rightly, then you are indeed a man of true wisdom.''[225] (Antoine de Saint Exupéry)

God's Word: Ps. 38.

Personal Reflection:

                                                                                13
_____

Wisdom consists of the anticipation of consequences.[226] (Norman Cousins)

God's Word: Prov. 1:20–33.

Personal Reflection:

                                                                                14
_____

Theme:

Truth – Faithful Lighthouse

Only the man who is firmly rooted in truth can establish peace, without insult and compromise.[227] (L. Boros)

God's Word: 1 Jn. 5:18–21.

Personal Reflection:

_____ **15**

So long as the love of God is not recognized and grasped as a primordial truth, our human experience lacks depth. It knows nothing of its principle and foundation.[228] (François Roustang)

God's Word: Col. 2:6–8.

Personal Reflection:

_____ **16**

There are times and circumstances, Chesterton jocosely said, when it is necessary to exaggerate in order to tell the truth.[229] (J. C. Murray)

God's Word: Mk. 13:1–4.

Personal Reflection:

_____ **17**

Gonzalo: My Lord, Sebastian,
The truth you speak doth lack some gentleness
And time to speak it in; you rub the sore,
When you should bring the plaster.[230] (Shakespeare)

God's Word: Hos. 2:1–13.

Personal Reflection:

18

It is the fact that falsehood is never so false as when it is very nearly true.[231] (G. K. Chesterton)

God's Word: Jn. 13:21–30.

Personal Reflection:

19

The beginning of love is truth, and before He [God] will give us His Love, God must cleanse our souls of the lies that are in them.[232] (Thomas Merton)

God's Word: Is. 1:10–20.

Personal Reflection:

20

Sometimes, indeed, he took in the facts you had stated; but truth fared none the better for that. What are facts without interpretation?[233] (C. S. Lewis)

God's Word: Mk. 4:13–20.

Personal Reflection:

21

Theme:

Person – Immortal Diamond

A new person is to me a great event and hinders me from sleep.[234] (Emerson)
God's Word: Gen. 29:9–14.

Personal Reflection:

_____ **22**

And for him the point is always that Man is not a balloon going up into the sky, nor a mole burrowing merely in the earth; but rather a thing like a tree, whose roots are fed from the earth, while its highest branches seem to rise almost to the stars.[235] (G. K. Chesterton)
God's Word: Jb. 29:18–20.

Personal Reflection:

_____ **23**

Prophecy has in its ways declared that the unique being, man, is created to be a centre of surprise in creation.[236] (Martin Buber)
God's Word: Sir. 17:1–4.

Personal Reflection:

_____ **24**

Miranda: O wonder!
How many goodly creatures are there here!
How beauteous mankind is! O brave new world,
That hath such people in 't![237] (Shakespeare)

God's Word: Gen. 1:26–31.

Personal Reflection:

25

"I know a planet where there is a certain red-faced gentleman. He has never smelled a flower. He has never looked at a star. He has never loved anyone. He has never done anything in his life but add up figures. And all day he says over and over, just like you: 'I am busy with matters of consequence!' And that makes him swell up with pride. But he is not a man—he is a mushroom!"[238] (Antoine de Saint Exupéry)

God's Word: Mk. 10:23–27.

Personal Reflection:

26

Let each person therefore have confidence in the individual nature which God had given him, let him find there the basis for his life and the path which is revealed to him leading him to God; let him not suffer any image to be imposed by somebody else or receive any measure from outside.[239] (Romano Guardini)

God's Word: Mt. 16:17–20.

Personal Reflection:

27

. . . the essence of being a "person" is surrendering oneself to another and finding fulfillment precisely in that other.[240] (Jon Sobrino)

God's Word: Jer. 18:1–6.

Personal Reflection:

28

Theme:

Creativity – Silent Butterfly

There are creative manners, there are creative actions, and creative words; manners, actions, words, that is, indicative of no custom or authority, but springing spontaneous from the mind's own sense of good and fair.[241] (Emerson)

God's Word: Gen. 1:1–5.

Personal Reflection:

29

. . . she must consciously encourage those pursuits which oppose the centrifugal forces of today. Quiet time alone, contemplation, prayer, music, a centering line of thought or reading, of study or work. It can be physical or intellectual or artistic, any creative life proceeding from oneself. It need not be an enormous project or a great work. But it should be something of one's own. Arranging a bowl of flowers in the morning can give a sense of quiet in a crowded day—like writing a poem, or saying a prayer. What matters is that one be for a time inwardly attentive.[242] (Anne Morrow Lindbergh)

God's Word: Jn. 12:1–8.

Personal Reflection:

30

Artistic paternity is as wholesome as physical paternity.[243] (G. K. Chesterton)

God's Word: Col. 1:15–20.

Personal Reflection:

31

SEPTEMBER

IT IS IN SEPTEMBER that the sky becomes more angry with the world, that teachers limber up their minds and reach for the oil can, that Saturdays speak of homecomings, that the sun begins to angle further to the south and west, that birds become restless and anticipate a move, that gnomes build extra rooms in preparation for winter, that fields breathe a sigh of relief after a race well run, that the lawn goes to the barber less often, that cemeteries seem to be more prominent, that cucumber vines are gathered for cremation, that cottages bid farewell to their guests, that fears shelved for some months mysteriously return, that joy haunts the heart at completion of work, that homesickness crushes the distant lad. *These have been some of my Septembers—what about yours?*

It is in September that certain questions run through my heart:
> whence influence?
>> why the power of home, friends, and land?
> whence spirituality?
>> why this deep longing for union with all reality?
> whence knowledge?
>> why do ideas delight and vision enthrall?
> whence insideness?
>> why this necessity for empathy and compassion?
> whence growth?
>> why do some people grow year after year and others remain "autumn-hatched birds"?

These have been some of my Septembers—what about yours?

IT WAS IN SEPTEMBER that certain lessons and insights came home: that peace is achieved only through love and order; that fallen apples tell of a universal law that boggles the mind; that education is a precious treasure to be nurtured through every phase of life; that summer procrastinations are never taken care of in the fall; that people love by giving themselves rather than by offering a gift; that fears are best dealt with through naming and ownership; that the sun's fidelity tells a beautiful story of a faithful God. *These have been some of my Septembers—what about yours?*

A September Poem

As imperceptibly as Grief
The Summer lapsed away—
Too imperceptible at last
To seem like Perfidy—
A Quietness distilled
As Twilight long begun,
Or Nature spending with herself
Sequestered Afternoon—
The Dusk drew earlier in—
The Morning foreign shone—
A courteous, yet harrowing Grace,
As Guest, that would be gone—
And thus, without a Wing
Or service of a Keel
Our Summer made her light escape
Into the Beautiful.

Emily Dickinson

Theme:

Influence – Vibrant Air

. . . for the influence of action is not to be measured in miles.[244] (Emerson)

God's Word: Is. 6:1–9.

Personal Reflection:

1

I will tell you a day in my life that has shaped me. . .[245] (C. S. Lewis)

God's Word: Lk. 5:12–14.

Personal Reflection:

2

As one idea will blossom from another,
So out of that, another thought arose.[246] (Dante)

God's Word: Mt. 10:26–31.

Personal Reflection:

                                                                                    3
_____

Plotinus, Paschal, Peguy, Bergson, Leon Bloy bathed our souls with their spiritual influence.[247]
(Raïssa Maritain)

God's Word: Acts. 4:1–22.

Personal Reflection:

                                                                                    4
_____

Nothing has a stronger influence psychologically on their environment, and especially on their
children, than the unlived life of the parents.[248] (C. G. Jung)

God's Word: Mt. 20:20–23.

Personal Reflection:

                                                                                    5
_____

An infection begun in the mind will reach every extremity.[249] (Walter Kerr)

God's Word: Sir. 10:6–18.

Personal Reflection:

                                                                                    6
_____

We leave traces of ourselves wherever we go, on whatever we touch.[250] (Lewis Thomas)

God's Word: Ps. 6.

Personal Reflection:

7

Theme:

Spirituality – Tenacious Roots

By spirituality I mean primarily how one relates to God and how he views himself and others as a result of this relationship. Everyone who believes in God lives according to some spirituality in the sense that he has received or developed some understanding of the Supreme Being and related to Him in terms of that understanding.[251] (John Haughey)

God's Word: Ps. 5.

Personal Reflection:

8

The perfect achievement of our spiritual life is dependent on the spiritual life of every other human being.[252] (François Roustang)

God's Word: Rom. 1:8–15.

Personal Reflection:

9

Do you know when people really become spiritual? It is when they become the slaves of God and are branded with His sign, which is the sign of the Cross, in token that they have given Him their freedom.[253] (Teresa of Avila)

God's Word: Phm. 1:1.

Personal Reflection:

10

We then find that any society that denies the individual the possibility of spiritual growth and freedom estranges one from oneself, regardless of its material conditions and educational maturity.[254] (Louis Dupré)

God's Word: Rom. 2:18–32.

Personal Reflection:

11

To live a spiritual life is to live in the presence of God.[255] (Henri Nouwen)

God's Word: Ps. 89.

Personal Reflection:

12

The cross is the most peculiar and distinctive feature of Christian faith, but Christian spirituality is not formally a spirituality of suffering: rather it is a spirituality focused on the following of Jesus.[256] (Jon Sobrino)

God's Word: Mt. 9:9.

Personal Reflection:

                                                                                          13

They [the saints] mean that love and desire constitute the life of the spirit.[257] *(The Cloud of Unknowing)*

God's Word: Rom. 8:28–30.

Personal Reflection:

                                                                                          14

Theme:

Knowledge – Northern Lights

For it is extraordinary what difference there is between understanding a thing and knowing it by experience.[258] (Teresa of Avila)

God's Word: 1 Jn. 2:3–11.

Personal Reflection:

_____ **15**

For who can know himself, and the multitude of subtle influences which act upon him?[259] (John Henry Newman)

God's Word: Ps. 71.

Personal Reflection:

_____ **16**

''I do not know at all,'' said Martin. ''I should have to be in your hearts to know.'' [260] (Voltaire)

God's Word: Dt. 6:4–9.

Personal Reflection:

_____ **17**

In science I missed the factor of meaning; and in religion, that of empiricism.[261] (C. G. Jung)

God's Word: Mk. 3:22–30.

Personal Reflection:

18

The longer I know you, the better I like you,
Beloved Beowulf.[262] (Beowulf)

God's Word: 1 Cor. 1:4–9.

Personal Reflection:

19

I have one outstanding trait in my character, which must strike anyone who knows me for any length of time, and that is my knowledge of myself. I can watch myself and my actions, just like an outsider. The Anne of every day I can face entirely without prejudice, without making excuses for her, and watch what's good and what's bad about her.[263] (Anne Frank)

God's Word: Ps. 106.

Personal Reflection:

20

The transcendence of experience and the transformation of fact into principle is the work of reason.[264] (J. C. Murray)

God's Word: Jn. 6:26–27.

Personal Reflection:

21

Theme:

Insideness – Mysterious Castle

A painter told me that nobody could draw a tree without in some sort becoming a tree; or draw a child by studying the outlines of its form merely—but by watching for a time his motions and plays, the painter enters into his nature and can then draw him at will in every attitude.[265] (Emerson)

God's Word: Mk. 11:12–14.

Personal Reflection:

22

Who can *feel* ugly when the heart meets delight? It is as if, somewhere inside, within the hideous face and bony limbs, one is soft, fresh, lissom and desirable.[266] (C. S. Lewis)

God's Word: Mt. 18:12–14.

Personal Reflection:

23

"I saw Him [God]. I did so," said the child.

"We will go and look all about," I comforted, "for that is good to do. But mostly we will look inside, for that is where we ache and where we laugh and where at last we die. I think it is most there that He is very close."[267] (Loren Eiseley)

God's Word: Jn. 14:23.

Personal Reflection:

24

What did vassals feel about those other totems, the lions or the leopards upon the shields of their lord? So long as we neglect this subjective side of history, which may more simply be called the inside of history, there will always be a certain limitation on that science which can be better transcended by art. So long as the historian cannot do that, fiction will be truer than fact. There will be more reality in a novel; yes, even in a historical novel.[268] (G. K. Chesterton)

God's Word: 1 Th. 5:15.

Personal Reflection:

25

Wherever there is a reaching down into innermost experience, into the nucleus of personality, most people are overcome by fright, and many run away . . . . The risk of inner experience, the adventure of the spirit, is in any case alien to most human beings.[269] (C. G. Jung)

God's Word: Ps. 27.

Personal Reflection:

26

He [Thomas Aquinas] always attempted to look at everything from the inside.[270] (G. K. Chesterton)

God's Word: Lk. 6:36–38.

Personal Reflection:

27

Nature also, where vital needs are in play, wipes out all interior life, even to a mother's sorrow.[271] (Simone Weil)

God's Word: Lk. 7:36–50.

Personal Reflection:

28

Theme:

Growth – Patient Redwood

We live in an age of impatience, an age which in everything, from learning the ABC to industry, tries to cut out and do away with the natural season of growth. That is why so much in our life is abortive.[272] (Caryll Houselander)

God's Word: Sir. 1:22–24.

Personal Reflection:

29

We are absolutely in need of our fellowmen to realize and to develop ourselves, so much so that the man who seeks to isolate himself in order not to have to acquire a unity that is difficult for him, no longer finds in himself the least substance; rather he finds only emptiness and absence.[273] (François Roustang)

God's Word: Mk. 3:13–19.

Personal Reflection:

30

OCTOBER

IT IS IN OCTOBER that the smoldering leaves scent the air with mysterious odors, that "sheer plod makes plough down sillion shine," that summer dreams are finally buried, that the marsh ponds become international airports, that football widows realize the permanence of their situation, that nurses prefer the corridors of the woods to their antiseptic halls, that students begin to sense flight or grounding, that an early snowflake arrives just to check future lodging, that a spring kite decides to challenge the autumn wind, that builders enclose their delicate work before the north-westerly arrives, that an August night returns to haunt the inner spirit with strange moods. *These have been some of my Octobers—what about yours?*

It is in October that certain questions run through my heart:

    where does the heart reside?
      why its constant demands for softening and care?
    whence affection?
      why is life arid, without deep sharing and feeling?
    whence fear?
      why the struggle against so many terrorizing demons?
    whence the self?
      why this mysterious mixture that defies analysis?
    whence intimacy?
      why this eternal pull toward oneness of mind, heart, and body?

These have been some of my Octobers—what about yours?

IT WAS IN OCTOBER that certain lessons and insights came home to me: that leaves must fall if spring is to come; that intimacy is the deepest and most profound longing of the human heart; that affirmation is a pivotal motivating factor in life; that we will never come to full knowledge of self on this journey; that time does stand still in the presence of a friend; that one hour in the woods is worth a week in the city; that death cannot be denied its own rhythm. *These have been some of my Octobers—what about yours?*

An October Poem

SPRING AND FALL:

to a young child

Margaret, are you grieving
Over Goldengrove unleaving?
Leaves, like the things of man, you
With your fresh thoughts care for, can you?
Ah! as the heart grows older
It will come to such sights colder
By and by, nor spare a sigh
Though worlds of wanwood leafmeal lie;
And yet you will weep and know why.
Now no matter, child, the name:
Sorrow's springs are the same.
Nor mouth had, no nor mind, expressed
What heart heard of, ghost guessed:
It is the blight man was born for,
It is Margaret you mourn for.

Gerard Manley Hopkins

Theme:

Heart – Life's Touchstone

"But I feel nothing," she whispered to herself. "I have no heart."[274] (Thornton Wilder)
God's Word: Is. 3:16–24.

Personal Reflection:

1

When your own heart's been broken it will be time for you to think of talking.[275] (C. S. Lewis)
God's Word: Is. 5:1–4.

Personal Reflection:

2

Pity me that the heart is slow to learn
What the swift mind beholds at every turn.[276]
(Edna St. Vincent Millay)
God's Word: Mk. 4:30–34.

Personal Reflection:

3

His sorrow will not be slight. His heart is proud and hard.[277] (H. Hesse)

God's Word: Ps. 14.

Personal Reflection:

    4

And near it, under a low dome, should be his tomb, with a Persian inscription:
    Alas, without me for thousands of years
    The Rose will blossom and the Spring will bloom,
    But those who have secretly understood my heart—
    They will approach and visit the grave where I lie.[278] (E. M. Forster)

God's Word: Jn. 20:1–10.

Personal Reflection:

    5

Certainly the heart has always something to tell about the future to those who listen to it.[279] (A. Manzoni)

God's Word: Prov. 14:33.

Personal Reflection:

    6

More: What you have hunted me for is not my actions, but the thoughts of my heart. It is a long road you have opened. For first men will disclaim their hearts and presently they will have no hearts. God help the people whose Statesmen walk your road.[280] (Robert Bolt)

God's Word: 1 Kg. 20:35–43.

Personal Reflection:

    7

Theme:

Affection – Healing Touch

Man's hairs are easier to count than his affections and the movements of his heart.[281] (Augustine)
God's Word: Sg. 4:1–10.

Personal Reflection:

8

Our intellectual and active powers increase with our affection.[282] (Emerson)
God's Word: Sir. 1:25–40.

Personal Reflection:

9

The truly wide taste in humanity will similarly find something to appreciate in the cross-section of humanity whom one has to meet every day. In my experience it is Affection that creates this taste, teaching us first to notice, then to endure, then to smile at, then to enjoy, and finally to appreciate, the people who "happen to be there."[283] (C. S. Lewis)
God's Word: 1 Pt. 1:22–24.

Personal Reflection:

10

In losing you, I lose what I can seldom expect to meet with—an affectionate heart.[284] (John Henry Newman)

God's Word: 2 Cor. 13:11–13.

Personal Reflection:

11

"Persons form *lasting* attachments far more by their views of things than their feelings", Newman said with his usual insight, when warning against haste in separation. With time and work, "the glow of affection cools—and they find themselves drawing nearer to others whom they did not like as well, in consequence of similarity of views with them."[285] (Meriol Trevor)

God's Word: Acts 15:36–40.

Personal Reflection:

12

The father was too kind in what he said about me; his affection blinded him a little.[286] (John XXIII)

God's Word: Gen. 27:1–17.

Personal Reflection:

13

I have no defense against affection; I could be bribed with a sardine.[287] (Teresa of Avila)

God's Word: Jn. 20:11–18.

Personal Reflection:

14

Theme:

Fear – Gloomy Clouds

But as often happens, just as a man who has had trouble with a poor physician fears to entrust himself even to a good one, so it was with my soul's health.[288] (Augustine)
God's Word: Mk. 9:14–29.

Personal Reflection:

15

We are afraid of truth, afraid of fortune, afraid of death, and afraid of each other.[289] (Emerson)
God's Word: Is. 41:14–16.

Personal Reflection:

16

These fears robbed me of much freedom of spirit.[290] (Teresa of Avila)
God's Word: Mt. 26:56.

Personal Reflection:

17

. . . for fear is inseparable from pride and lust.[291] (Thomas Merton)

God's Word: Mt. 1:16–18.

Personal Reflection:

18

"I will have no man in my boat," said Starbuck, "who is not afraid of a whale." By this, he seemed to mean, not only that the most reliable and useful courage was that which arises from the fair estimation of the encountered peril, but that an utterly fearless man is a far more dangerous comrade than a coward.[292] (Melville)

God's Word: Sir. 1:11–20.

Personal Reflection:

19

Young Mortimer: Fear'd am I more than lov'd; let me be fear'd,
and when I frown, make all the court look pale.[293] (Christopher Marlowe)

God's Word: Mk. 15:1–15.

Personal Reflection:

20

One should be fearful only of those things
Which have the power to harm one's fellow men.[294] (Dante)

God's Word: Lk. 12:4–7.

Personal Reflection:

21

Theme:

Self – Honest Mirror

We must be our own before we can be another's.[295] (Emerson)

God's Word: 1 Tim. 3:1–7.

Personal Reflection:

_____ **22**

When He [God] talks of their losing their selves, He means only abandoning the clamour of self-will.[296] (C. S. Lewis)

God's Word: Mk. 8:35.

Personal Reflection:

_____ **23**

One of the most astonishing facts about the human animal is that you can meet someone for 20 minutes and discern more about what makes him tick than he has learned about himself in 40 years; and, of course, so can he about you.[297] (S. J. Harris)

God's Word: Sir. 18:19–29.

Personal Reflection:

_____ **24**

The ego is an obstacle to vision and possession.[298] (Raïssa Maritain)

God's Word: 1 Sam. 15:24–31.

Personal Reflection:

25

The "self behind the frontage," it has been observed, is in all of us something greater than the self of the shop-window which all the world can see.[299] (C. H. Dodd)

God's Word: Acts 9:1–19.

Personal Reflection:

26

It is not my business to think about myself. My business is to think about God. It is for God to think about me.[300] (Simone Weil)

God's Word: Ps. 103.

Personal Reflection:

27

Thomas More: When a man takes an oath, Meg, he's holding his own self in his own hands. Like water. (He cups his hands) And if he opens his fingers *then*—he needn't hope to find himself again. Some aren't capable of this, but I'd be loathe to think your father one of them.[301] (Robert Bolt)

God's Word: Ex. 32:13–14.

Personal Reflection:

28

Theme:

Intimacy – Gracious Embrace

To love at all is to be vulnerable. Love anything, and your heart will certainly be wrung and possibly be broken. If you want to make sure of keeping it intact, you must give your heart to no one, not even to an animal. Wrap it carefully round with hobbies and little luxuries; avoid all entanglements; lock it up safe in the casket or coffin of your selfishness. But in that casket—safe, dark, motionless, airless—it will change. It will not be broken; it will become unbreakable, impenetrable, irredeemable. The alternative to tragedy, or at least to the risk of tragedy, is damnation. The only place outside Heaven where you can be perfectly safe from all the dangers and perturbations of love is Hell.[302] (C. S. Lewis)

God's Word: Jn. 15:7–12.

Personal Reflection:

29

Being open to intimacy depends on a strong identity, including a firm sense of our sexual identity.[303] (Gail Sheehy)

God's Word: Rom. 13:8–10.

Personal Reflection:

30

Everybody knows that really intimate conversation is only possible between two or three. As soon as there are six or seven, collective language begins to dominate. That is why it is a complete misinterpretation to apply to the Church the words "Wheresoever them." Christ did not say two hundred, or fifty, or ten. He said two or three. He said precisely that he always forms the third in the intimacy of the tête-à-tête.[304] (Simone Weil)

God's Word: Jn. 4:15–26.

Personal Reflection:

31

NOVEMBER

IT IS IN NOVEMBER that the turkey puzzles over the joy of a day of thanksgiving, that special trips are made to the cemetery, filled now with leaves, that Christmas decorations are displayed too soon, that the forest seduces the human heart, that golf clubs retire and racquetballs begin their dance, that poor souls become rich depending upon 6-6-6, that the Church year ends with apocalyptic fear, that skiers find it hard to sleep with the smell of snow in the air, that static electricity surprises us at every touch, that gifts are recognized for what they are, that meaning must be found for large questions. *These have been some of my Novembers—what about yours?*

It is in November that certain questions run through my heart:

whence evil?

why do pain, chaos, and disorder seem to dominate much of life?

whence experience?

why do we distance ourselves from the heart of reality—are most velveteen rabbits now extinct?

whence speaking?

why does the human word bring so much joy and pain?

whence sympathy?

why are we blessed with a gentle heart and listening spirit?

whence weakness?

why is there a paradox that makes us strong in our vulnerability?

These have been some of my Novembers—what about yours?

IT WAS IN NOVEMBER that certain lessons and insights came home to me: that a kind, gentle word is one of the most powerful forces in the universe; that ninety percent of evil can be traced back to freedom misused; that experience at bottom is a matter of the heart; that weakness is often our strongest gift; that people do remember the dead; that love and work need careful balancing; that peace can be experienced deep within while the surface of life is in turmoil. *These have been some of my Novembers—what about yours?*

A November Poem

MY NOVEMBER GUEST

My Sorrow, when she's here with me,
  Thinks these dark days of autumn rain
Are beautiful as days can be;
She loves the bare, the withered tree;
  She walks the sodden pasture lane.

Her pleasure will not let me stay.
  She talks and I am fain to list:
She's glad the birds are gone away,
She's glad her simple worsted gray
  Is silver now with clinging mist.

The desolate, deserted trees,
  The faded earth, the heavy sky,
The beauties she so truly sees,
She thinks I have no eye for these,
  And vexes me for reason why.

Not yesterday I learned to know
  The love of bare November days
Before the coming of the snow,
But it were vain to tell her so,
  And they are better for her praise.

Robert Frost

Theme:

Evil – Brooding Witches

Thus in this ancient and wonderful poem [Iliad] there already appears the essential evil besetting humanity, the substitution of means for ends.[305] (Simone Weil)

God's Word: Sir. 11:29–34.

Personal Reflection:

_____ **1**

I asked, "What is iniquity?" and I found that it is not a substance. It is perversity of will, twisted away from the supreme substance. . .[306] (Augustine)

God's Word: Ps. 83.

Personal Reflection:

_____ **2**

There are some things no man can face.[307] (C. S. Lewis)

God's Word: Mt. 14:66–73.

Personal Reflection:

_____ **3**

They (historians, moralists, philosophers) form no idea of essential evil, that vast yearning for the void, for emptiness; since if ever our species is to perish it will die of boredom, of stale disgust.[308] (G. Bernanos)

God's Word: Prov. 14:10.

Personal Reflection:

4

"And you, sometimes you are a snake, and sometimes a whisper, and again, a daydream, a lump in the blood, a sweet face, an ambition, a scheme for making money, a task for an army. Sometimes you can even be a man and disarm everyone entirely who cannot see your heart. But someone there is who always sees. Goodness is often performed without the slightest knowledge of its doing. But evil is always known."[309] (Paul Horgan)

God's Word: 2 Pt. 2:11–22.

Personal Reflection:

5

How abolish an evil without first having clearly perceived in what it consisted?[310] (Simone Weil)

God's Word: 1 Jn. 1:8–10.

Personal Reflection:

6

But we mortals are generally like that: we rebel furiously and violently against mediocre evils, and bow down in silence under extreme ones; we endure, not from resignation but from stupidity, the very extremes of what we had at first called quite unendurable.[311] (A. Manzoni)

God's Word: Mt. 18:21–35.

Personal Reflection:

7

Theme:

Experience – Vital
            Heartbeat

. . . the reason can testify only inadequately to things of which it has no experience.[312] (Teresa of Avila)

God's Word: Heb. 11:1–3.

Personal Reflection:

8

I do not need any hope of any promise in order to believe that God is rich in mercy. I know this wealth of his with the certainty of experience; I have touched it.[313] (Simone Weil)

God's Word: Ps. 65.

Personal Reflection:

9

No one has any obligation to a concept; that is what is so agreeable about conceptuality—it promises protection from experience. The spirit does not dwell in concepts, but in deeds and in facts. Words butter no parsnips; nevertheless, this futile procedure is repeated *ad infinitum*.[314] (C. G. Jung)

God's Word: Jam. 1:19–27.

Personal Reflection:

10

Boatman: From Richmond to Chelsea, a penny halfpenny . . . from Chelsea to Richmond, a penny halfpenny. From Richmond to Chelsea, it's a quiet float downstream, from Chelsea to Richmond, it's a hard pull upstream. And it's a penny halfpenny either way. Whoever makes the regulations doesn't row a boat.[315] (Robert Bolt)

God's Word: Mk. 7:1–11.

Personal Reflection:

11

St. Anselm of Canterbury, in his profound work entitled *Proslogium*, says ''Without experience, no knowledge; but without faith, no experience.''[316] (Romano Guardini)

God's Word: Jn. 6:52–66.

Personal Reflection:

12

He hasn't been there—not lately, perhaps not ever.[317] (Walter Kerr)

God's Word: Ps. 91.

Personal Reflection:

13

. . . for a thing which cannot be experienced may easily be suspected of non-existence.[318] (C. G. Jung)

God's word: 1 Jn. 5:5–12.

Personal Reflection:

14

Theme:

Speaking – Mixed Arrows

A man cannot speak but he judges himself. With his will or against his will he draws his portrait to the eye of his companions by every word.[319] (Emerson)

God's Word: Lk. 6:43–45.

Personal Reflection:

15

Jill held her tongue. (If you don't want other people to know how frightened you are, this is always a wise thing to do; it's your voice that gives you away.)[320] (C. S. Lewis)

God's Word: Lk. 17:11–19.

Personal Reflection:

16

"Hold thy peace, dear little Pearl!" whispered her mother. "We must not always talk in the market-place of what happens to us in the forest."[321] (Hawthorne)

God's Word: Sir. 20:1–8.

Personal Reflection:

17

Absolute: You blockhead, never say more than is necessary.[322] (Sheridan)

God's Word: Sir. 7:14–15.

Personal Reflection:

18

Just as much as the young one wants to drink, the old man wants to talk. It will soon be a week since his son died, and he has not been able to speak about it properly to anyone.[323] (Chekhov)

God's Word: Lk. 24:9–11.

Personal Reflection:

19

But, in great as in little things, this long and winding path could be avoided by following the method laid down for so long, of observing, listening, comparing, and thinking before speaking. But speaking is in itself so much easier than all the others put together, that we, too—I mean we humans in general—are a little to be pitied.[324] (A. Manzoni)

God's Word: Jude 1:8–10.

Personal Reflection:

_____ **20**

. . . one speaks badly of the intimate depths of the spirit if one does not do so with a deeply recollected soul.[325] (John of the Cross)

God's Word: 1 Tm. 4:16.

Personal Reflection:

_____ **21**

Theme:

Sympathy – Inner Tears

"Ah!" croaked the Raven. "It is an old saying: see the bear in his own den before you judge of his conditions."[326] (C. S. Lewis)

God's Word: Sir 7:11–12.

Personal Reflection:

22

I can think of my debt to you, and when you are tempted to be low and despondent, if such feelings ever come on you, as if you were lonely and desolate, do recollect that there is one at a distance who is thinking of you and praying for you; and into whose eyes tears start at the thought of your having any sorrow or perplexity, especially through him. O what a world is this, and how great are its trials—and none duly knows them but He whose blessed will imposes them, and who can turn them all to blessings.[327] (John Henry Newman)

God's Word: 1 Pt. 1:3–9.

Personal Reflection:

23

These are myths: and he who has no sympathy with myths has no sympathy with men.[328] (G. K. Chesterton)

God's Word: Lk. 15:4–7.

Personal Reflection:

24

. . . that, finally, to this poor pilgrim, on his dreary and desert path, faint, sick, miserable, there appeared a glimpse of human affection and sympathy, a new life, and a true one, in exchange for the heavy doom which he was now expiating.[329] (Hawthorne)

God's Word: Ps. 69.

Personal Reflection:

25

She could scarcely bear the thought, yet for so many years she had not only feared but also condemned them, had actually "disdained their misery," telling herself it was their fault. Yes, she, detestable, fear-enslaved Much-Afraid had actually dared to disdain them for the things which made them so wretched and ugly when she herself was equally wretched and enslaved. Instead of a fellow-feeling of compassion and passionate desire that they might be delivered and transformed from the pride and resentment and bitterness which made them what they were, she had just detested and despised them.[330] (H. Hurnard)

God's Word: Qo. 10:8–9.

Personal Reflection:

26

Supposing that we cannot give a cure, we can still give sympathy, and "this means sharing in another's sorrow, a real self-giving. Anything else can be given without involving self, but sympathy *is* giving self to suffer someone else's suffering."[331] (Maisie Ward, quoting Caryll Houselander)

God's Word: Mk. 7:31–37.

Personal Reflection:

27

Here I saw part of the compassion of our Lady, St. Mary; for Christ and she were so united in love that the greatness of her love was the cause of the greatness of her pain.[332] (Julian of Norwich)

God's Word: Jn. 19:25–27.

Personal Reflection:

28

Theme:

Weakness – Bruised Apple

Later, no doubt, the time in which I am now will appear to me still full of imperfections, but now I am no longer astonished at anything. I am not troubled at seeing that I am weakness itself. On the contrary it is in that that I glory and each day I expect to discover fresh imperfections in myself. Remembering that Charity covers a multitude of sins, I draw from this rich mine which Jesus opened before me.[333] (Teresa of Lisieux)

God's Word: Ph. 4:10–13.

Personal Reflection:

29

It seems that upon entering the world, God renounced his omnipotence; he, Truth, left his mantle of irresistibility outside the gates of earth, in order to enter in a form that would permit people to close their hearts to him if they so desired. Purposely God limited his illimitable radiance, wrapping himself in a darkness which enabled men to withstand and even to reject his rays. Perhaps in imposing these limitations on himself, God was conforming to the weakness of the creatures to whom he descended.[334] (Romano Guardini)

God's Word: Heb. 5:1–10.

Personal Reflection:

30

DECEMBER

IT IS IN DECEMBER that evergreens wander in from the fields to be dressed in regal lights, that loneliness can be sensed for miles around, that rivers and lakes are transformed and people once again walk on water, that long-johns have a felt significance, that deer from deep swamps emerge, knowing the protection of law, that whispers of Santa Claus are heard around the chimney, that cynics voice their frozen cry of bah-humbug, that Handel revisits the earth—alleluia, that the nutcracker brings joy to the spirit, that at least for one night all is silent. *These have been some of my Decembers— what about yours?*

It is in December that certain questions run through my heart:

> whence worlds?
>> why so many stars with their planets and eyes with their thoughts?
>
> whence action?
>> why all this energy to do and to change?
>
> whence writing?
>> why take pen in hand and record the movements of the heart and mind?
>
> whence environment?
>> why these climates of growth or regression?
>
> whence expectations?
>> why so many desires and hopes in such a fragile world?

These have been some of my Decembers—what about yours?

IT WAS IN DECEMBER that certain lessons and insights came home: that we truly had better watch out, we had better not cry; that for every death there is a new life; that waiting can be as meaningful as finding; that Captain Midnight isn't such a bad guy after all; that the North Pole of the human heart has its own season; that hockey pucks are an instrument of joy and pain; that, given the proper temperature, snow does sing; that a burning log is a symbol of all life. *These have been some of my Decembers— what about yours?*

A December Poem

Star in clear winter sky seems
    to grow dim
  in its apparent struggle
    to reach earth
  with its message
while bare, stark tree appears
    to outstretch its branches
  in its creaking attempt
    to touch heaven
  with its presence.
Like both of these
    man is sometimes asked
  to catch the moon
while standing upon the ground
      or
    to illuminate the world
  as evening shadows close in.
     Either can be done,
but it takes
  belief
    trust
      much caring
  to overcome a reality
which, after all this,
  perhaps only exists
    in the worlds of
     all those stars
that have never shone,
    all those trees
that have never grown.

Barbara J. Holt

Theme:

World – Swirling Planets

She told him her story as they walked. In his company she had that curious sensation which most married people know of being with someone whom (for the final but wholly mysterious reason) one could never have married but who is nevertheless more of one's own world than the person one has married in fact.[335] (C. S. Lewis)

God's Word: Jn. 4:27–30.

Personal Reflection:

                                                                                                    1

Oh, I'd give anything—I wonder why you can get into our world and we can never get into yours?[336] (C. S. Lewis)

God's Word: Mt. 19:16–22.

Personal Reflection:

                                                                                                    2

As I went down the hill in the gathering darkness, I shivered. Old Mullens had lived in a small, tight world of marvels, and they had lasted him till the end. Never by word or deed had we intruded upon his beliefs.[337] (Loren Eiseley)

God's Word: Prov. 14:31.

Personal Reflection:

3

There is a religious war when two worlds meet; that is, when two visions of the world meet; or in more modern language when two moral atmospheres meet. What is the one man's breath is the other man's poison; and it is vain to talk of giving a pestilence a place in the sun.[338] (G. K. Chesterton)

God's Word: Rev. 19:11–21.

Personal Reflection:

4

But they are both right; if I may say so, it is a privilege of people who contradict each other in their cosmos to be both right.[339] (G. K. Chesterton)

God's Word: Prov. 24:3.

Personal Reflection:

5

The great world was but a rumor here, and, by the time it came to the brush deserts, mostly wrong. But a world, without limits of dimension dwelt behind the eyes of all those parched, brown people obedient to the natural terms of their lives. It was the world of the human soul, in which could live promises so beautiful and satisfactions so full of ease that the hardships and the betrayals of impersonal nature could be survived, if only someone came from time to time with the greatest news in all life.[340] (Paul Horgan)

God's Word: Rev. 22:1–15.

Personal Reflection:

6

A man who has been in another world does not come back unchanged.[341] (C. S. Lewis)

God's Word: Acts 2:14–36.

Personal Reflection:

7

Theme:

Action – Bold Stallion

. . . A seasoned warrior
Must know the difference between words and deeds.[342] (Beowulf)

God's Word: 1 Jn. 3:17–20.

Personal Reflection:

8

No matter how much faculty of idle seeing a man has, the step from knowing to doing is rarely taken.[343] (Emerson)

God's Word: Lk. 8:11–15.

Personal Reflection:

9

They cannot go on forever standing on one leg, or sitting without a chair, or walking with their legs tied, or grazing, like Tityrus's stags, on the air. Premises imply conclusions; germs lead to development; principles have issues; doctrines lead to action.[344] (John Henry Newman)

God's Word: 1 Pt. 3:8–12.

Personal Reflection:

10

If you have understood me, act at once![345] (Dante)

God's Word: Jn. 13:1–15.

Personal Reflection:

11

He knew a path that wanted walking;
He knew a spring that wanted drinking;
A thought that wanted further thinking;
A love that wanted re-renewing.
Nor was this just a way of talking
To save him the expense of doing,
With him it boded action, deed.[346] (Robert Frost)

God's Word: Lk. 4:42.

Personal Reflection:

12

Old Woman: I should like to know which is worse, to be raped a hundred times by . . . pirates, to have a buttock cut off . . . to be whipped and flogged in an *auto-da-fé*, to be dissected, to row in a galley, in short, to endure all the miseries through which we have passed, or to remain here doing nothing?''[347] (Voltaire)

God's Word: Ex. 32: 1–6.

Personal Reflection:

_____ **13**

Macbeth: This deed I'll do before this purpose cool.[348] (Shakespeare)

God's Word: Mt. 26:14–16.

Personal Reflection:

_____ **14**

Theme:

Writing – Friendly Pen

We write from aspiration and antagonism, as well as from experience. We paint those qualities which we do not possess. The poet admires the man of energy and tactics; the merchant breeds his son for the church or the bar; and where a man is not vain and egotistic you shall find what he has not by his praise.[349] (Emerson)

God's Word: Eph. 4:17–32.

Personal Reflection:

15

I should speak instead of write did it not hurt me to use my voice. Written words are harsher than spoken, so you must make allowances as you read on.[350] (John Henry Newman)

God's Word: Ex. 32:15–16.

Personal Reflection:

16

Learn as much by writing as by reading.[351] (Lord Acton)

God's Word: Rev. 1:1–3.

Personal Reflection:

17

All my writings may be considered tasks imposed from within; their source was a fateful compulsion. What I wrote were things that assailed me from within myself. I permitted the spirit that moved me to speak out. I have never counted upon any strong response, any powerful resonance, to my writings. They represent a compensation for our times, and I have been impelled to say what no one wants to hear.[352] (C. G. Jung)

God's Word: Jn. 21:24–25.

Personal Reflection:

18

At all events I had better continue the experiment to the end [diary]—I mean at least for several weeks. I will even force myself to write exactly what comes into my mind, without picking and choosing (sometimes I still search for words, correct myself), then I'll stuff it all away in a drawer and re-read it later with a clear mind.[353] (G. Bernanos)

God's Word: Gal. 1:19–24.

Personal Reflection:

19

And now I come to the root of the matter, the reason for my starting a diary; it is that I have no such real friendship.[354] (Anne Frank)

God's Word: Sg. 8:5–7.

Personal Reflection:

20

. . . he [Wordsworth] had written longer than he was inspired.[355] (Emerson)
God's Word: Prov. 31:1–31.

Personal Reflection:

_____   **21**

Theme:

Environment – Cozy Home

There is an environment of minds as well as space.[356] (C. S. Lewis)
God's Word: Acts 2:42–47.

Personal Reflection:

_____   **22**

Milton: I should have left you on your farm in Oxfordshire. You were a country plant, and withered in town.[357] (Don Taylor)

God's Word: 1 Sam. 16:14–23.

Personal Reflection:

23

. . . during the whole of that agitating, memorable week, there had been the extraordinary autumn weather that always comes as a surprise, when the sun hangs low and gives more heat than in spring, when everything shines so brightly in the rare clear atmosphere that the eyes smart, when the lungs are strengthened and refreshed by inhaling the aromatic autumn air, when even the nights are warm, and when in those dark warm nights, golden stars startle and delight us continually by falling from the sky.[358] (Tolstoy)

God's Word: Lk. 21:29–33.

Personal Reflection:

24

But he could not stir them. It was a dinner without a soul. For no reason that was clear to Babbitt, heaviness was over them and they spoke laboriously and unwillingly.[359] (Sinclair Lewis)

God's Word: Mk. 14:17–21.

Personal Reflection:

25

Fatigue and despair nibble away our good intentions. Lack of a night's sleep can destroy a resolution against peevishness; business troubles consume kindness. Saints master their environment as we do not.[360] (Phyllis McGinley)

God's Word: Ex. 32:30–35.

Personal Reflection:

26

Persons with any weight of character carry, like planets, their atmosphere along with them in their orbits; and the matron who entered now upon the scene could, and usually did, bring her own tone into a company.[361] (Thomas Hardy)

God's Word: Acts 15:8–12.

Personal Reflection:

27

The Being of God, then, presses upon man. It is his environment. It sings to him in the winds. When he touches grass or water, he touches it with his fingers; he smells it in fields of hay and clover and in newly cut wood; he listens to it in the falling of the rain and the murmur of the sea.[362] (Caryll Houselander)

God's Word: Ps. 100.

Personal Reflection:

28

Theme:

Expectation – Winter Dreams

Miss Hardcastle: You taught me to expect something extraordinary, and I find the original exceeds the description.[363] (Goldsmith)

God's Word: 1 Cor. 15:50–53.

Personal Reflection:

29

I compared notes with one of my friends who expects everything of the universe and is disappointed when anything is less than the best, and I found that I begin at the other extreme, expecting nothing, and am always full of thanks for moderate goods.[364] (Emerson)

God's Word: Mk. 14:3–9.

Personal Reflection:

30

One should be, as our Lord said, "Like people always on the watch, expecting their Lord." Expectant people are watchful, always looking for him they expect, always ready to find him in whatever comes along; however strange it may be, they always think he might be in it. This is what awareness of the Lord is to be like and it requires diligence that taxes a man's senses and powers to the utmost, if he is to achieve it and to take God evenly in all things—if he is to find God as much in one thing as in another.[365] (Meister Eckhart)

God's Word: Jn. 21:1–14.

Personal Reflection:

31

ENDNOTES

[1]Alessandro Manzoni, *The Betrothed*, translated by Daniel J. Connor (New York: The Macmillan Company, 1926), p. 489.

[2]William Blake, "A Poison Tree," *Poems of William Blake*, selected by Amelia H. Munson (New York: Thomas Y. Crowell Company, 1964), p. 69.

[3]C. S. Lewis, *The Screwtape Letters* (New York: Macmillan Publishing Co., Inc., 1961), p. 95.

[4]*The Confessions of St. Augustine*, translated by John K. Ryan, Book 2, Chapter 6 (New York: Image Books, 1960), p. 72.

[5]John Steinbeck, *The Grapes of Wrath* (New York: Macmillan Company, 1926), p. 47.

[6]William Shakespeare, *King Lear*, Act 2, Scene 2, lines 74-77, in *The Complete Works of William Shakespeare*, edited by William Aldis Wright, (Garden City, NY: Doubleday Doran & Co., Inc., 1936), p. 996.

[7]Antoine de Saint-Exupéry, *The Little Prince* (New York: Harcourt, Brace & World, 1943), p. 11.

[8]Ralph Waldo Emerson, "Gifts," *The Selected Writings of Ralph Waldo Emerson*, edited, with a biographical introduction by Brooks Atkinson (New York: Random House, 1940), p. 403.

[9]*The Confessions of St. Augustine*, Book 13, Chapter 26, p. 362.

[10]*The Complete Works of St. John of the Cross*, translated by Kieran Kavanaugh, O.C.D. and Otilio Rodriguez, O.C.D. (Washington, D.C.: ICS Publications, Institute of Carmelite Studies, 1973), p. 599.

[11]Jon Sobrino, S.J., *Christology at the Crossroads*, translated by John Drury (New York: Orbis Books, 1978), p. 281.

[12]*The Confessions of St. Augustine*, Book 1, Chapter 20, p. 63.

[13]Emerson, "Spiritual Laws," p. 206.

[14]*The Complete Works of St. Teresa of Jesus*, translated and edited by E. Allison Peers, I (New York: Sheed and Ward, 1944), p. 237.

[15]*Ibid.*, p. 192.

[16]John Henry Newman, *Apologia Pro Vita Sua* (Boston: The Riverside Press Cambridge, 1966), p. 36.

[17]C. S. Lewis, *Till We Have Faces* (Grand Rapids, MI: Wm. B. Eerdmans Publishing Company, 1956), p. 236.

[18]Loren Eiseley, *The Night Country* (New York: Scribner, 1973), p. 112.

[19]Carl G. Jung, *Memories, Dreams, Reflections*, recorded and edited by Aniela Jaffe, translated from the German by Richard and Clara Winston (New York: Vintage Books, 1965), p. 356.

[20]*The Grapes of Wrath*, p. 447.

[21]*Anne Frank: The Diary of a Young Girl*, translated from the Dutch by B. M. Mooyaart-Doubleday (New York: Doubleday & Company, Inc., 1952), p. 139.

[22]C. S. Lewis, *Out of the Silent Planet* (New York: The Macmillan Company, 1965), p. 101.

[23]Emerson, "Character," p. 377.

[24]G. K. Chesterton, *The Everlasting Man* (New York: A Doubleday Image Book, 1955), p. 93.

[25]Sir James Barrie.

[26]Richard Brinsley Sheridan, *The Rivals,* Act 1, Scene 2, edited by Vincent F. Hopper and Gerald B. Lahey (New York: Barron's Educational Series, 1958), p. 71.

[27]Beowulf: *The Oldest English Epic,* translated by Charles W. Kennedy (New York: Oxford University Press, 1968), lines 120–122, p. 6.

[28]*The Little Prince,* p. 18.

[29]Robert Frost, "Fire and Ice," *Complete Poems of Robert Frost,* (New York: Henry Holt and Company, 1949), p. 268.

[30]*The Screwtape Letters,* p. ix.

[31]Christopher Marlowe, *Dr. Faustus,* Act 2, Scene 1, lines 114–128, in *The Plays of Christopher Marlowe,* edited by Leo Kirschbaum (New York: The World Publishing Company, 1962), p. 355.

[32]Emerson, "Spiritual Laws," p. 194.

[33]C. S. Lewis, *The Horse and His Boy* (New York: The Macmillan Company, 1954), p. 36.

[34]Voltaire, *Candide and Other Writings,* edited by Haskell M. Block (New York: Modern Library, 1956), p. 155.

[35]Shakespeare, *Macbeth,* Act 1, Scene 7, lines 33–34, p. 1032.

[36]Dante Alighieri, *The Divine Comedy,* translated by Lawrence Grant White (New York: Pantheon Books, 1948), p. 7.

[37]Robert Frost, "The Death of the Hired Man," *Complete Poems of Robert Frost,* p. 52.

[38]Raïssa Maritain, *We Have Been Friends Together* (New York: Longmans, Green and Company, 1942), p. 77.

[39]C. S. Lewis, *That Hideous Strength* (New York: The Macmillan Company, 1946), p. 306.

[40]C. S. Lewis, *Mere Christianity* (New York: The Macmillan Company, 1947), p. 116.

[41]Gerald Vann, *St. Thomas Aquinas* (Chicago: Benziger Brothers, 1940), p. 161.

[42]C. S. Lewis, *A Grief Observed* (New York: The Seabury Press, 1961), p. 57.

[43]Statement by John Henry Newman, in Meriol Trevor, *Newman: Light in Winter* (Garden City: Doubleday, 1963), p. 540.

[44]Shakespeare, *King Lear,* Act 1, Scene 1, line 56, p. 984.

[45]William Blake, "The Little Black Boy," *Poems of William Blake,* p. 50.

[46]Thornton Wilder, *The Bridge of San Luis Rey* (New York: Washington Square Press, Inc., 1955), p. 107.

[47]C. S. Lewis, *A Grief Observed,* p.21.

[48]Whittaker Chambers, *Witness* (New York: Random House, 1952), p. 9.

[49]Christopher Marlowe, *Dr. Faustus,* Act 5, Scene 1, line 80, in *The Plays of Christopher Marlowe,* p. 70.

[50]Emerson, "The Over-Soul," p. 261.

[51]G. K. Chesterton, *The Everlasting Man,* p. 243.

[52]Sobrino, *Christology at the Crossroads,* p. 101.

[53]G. K. Chesterton, *St. Francis of Assisi* (New York: Doubleday and Company, 1924), p. 78.

[54]C. S. Lewis, *Surprised by Joy* (New York: Harcourt, Brace & World, Inc., 1955), p. 21.

[55]Fynn, *Mister God, This Is Anna* (New York: Holt, Rinehart and Winston, 1974), p. 36.

[56]*Raïssa's Journal,* presented by Jacques Maritain (Albany, New York: Magi Books, Inc., 1963), p. 225.

[57]*The Complete Works of St. John of the Cross,* p. 434.

[58]*The Complete Works of St. Teresa of Jesus,* II, p. 98.

[59]Sobrino, *Christology at the Crossroads,* p. 121.

[60]C. S. Lewis, *The Weight of Glory and Other Addresses* (Grand Rapids, MI: William B. Eerdmans Publishing Company, 1949), p. 39.

[61]*Beowulf,* lines 2890–2891, p. 92.

[62]Norman Cousins.

[63]Robert Bolt, *A Man for All Seasons* (New York: Random House, 1960), p. 150.

[64]*The Complete Works of St. John of the Cross,* p. 451.

[65]John Webster, *The Duchess of Malfi,* Act 5, Scene 3, line 18, edited by Vincent F. Hopper and Gerald B. Lahey (Woodbury, New York: Barron's Educational Series, 1960), p. 198.

[66]Paul Horgan, *A Devil in the Desert* (New York: Longmans, Green & Company, 1952), p. 58.

[67]Jean Montaurier, *A Passage Through Fire* (New York: Henry Holt and Company, 1965), p. 341.

[68]*The Confessions,* Book 10, Chapter 23, p. 252.

[69]*The Complete Works of St. Teresa,* I, pp. 313–314.

[70]C. S. Lewis, *Till We Have Faces,* p. 306.

[71]Georges Bernanos, *The Diary of a Country Priest,* translated by Pamela Morris (New York: Doubleday & Company, Inc., 1954), p. 184.

[72]Dante Alighieri, *The Divine Comedy,* p. 184.

[73]*The Simone Weil Reader,* edited by George A. Panichas (New York: David McKay Company, Inc., 1977), p. 48.

[74]Walter Kerr, *The Decline of Pleasure* (New York: Simon and Schuster, 1962), p. 273.

[75]Carl G. Jung, *Memories, Dreams, Reflections,* pp. 32–33.

[76]Dante Alighieri, *The Divine Comedy,* p. 98.

[77]Albert Camus, quoted in *Know or Listen to Those Who Know,* edited by John W. Gardner and Francesca Gardner Reese (New York: W. W. Norton & Company, Inc., 1975), p. 216.

[78]C. S. Lewis, *The Voyage of the Dawn Treader* (New York: The Macmillan Company, 1954), p. 162.

[79]*The Simone Weil Reader,* p. 62.

[80]*The Complete Works of St. John of the Cross,* p. 80.

[81]Emerson, "History," p. 128.

[82]G. K., Chesterton, The Everlasting Man, p. 153.

[83]Leo Tolstoy, *War and Peace,* translated by Louise and Aylmer Maude (New York: Simon and Schuster, 1942), p. 444.

[84]Emerson, "Spiritual Laws," pp. 198–199.

[85]Shakespeare, *King Lear,* Act 4, Scene 2, line 38, p. 1011.

[86]*The Confessions,* Book 7, Chapter 16, p. 174.

[87]Emerson, "Experience," p. 345.

[88]Ladislaus Boros, *Hidden God,* translated by Erika Young (New York: The Seabury Press, 1971), p. 9.

[89]Dante Alighieri, *The Divine Comedy,* p.142.

[90]Thomas Green, S. J., *When the Well Runs Dry* (Notre Dame, Indiana: Ave Maria Press, 1979), p. 97.

[91]Julian of Norwich, *Showings,* translated by Edmund Colledge, O.S.A. and James Walsh, S. J. (New York: Paulist Press, 1978), p. 183.

[92]Sören Kierkegaard, *Philosophical Fragments,* translated by David Swenson (New Jersey: Princeton University Press, 1962), p. 64.

[93]Henrik Ibsen, *Hedda Gabler,* Act 2, in *Eleven Plays of Henrik Ibsen* (New York: Modern Library, n.d.), p. 542.

[94]*The Simone Weil Reader,* p. 64.

[95]John Webster, *The Duchess of Malfi,* Act 3, Scene 5, p. 156.

[96]Paul Horgan, *A Distant Trumpet* (New York: Farrar, Straus & Cudahy, 1951), p. 10.

[97]Gerald Vann, *St. Thomas Aquinas*, p. 24.

[98]Emerson, ''Self-Reliance,'' p. 157.

[99]Emerson, ''Experience,'' p. 354.

[100]G. K. Chesterton, *The Everlasting Man*, p. 255.

[101]Paul Horgan, *Memories of the Future* (New York: Farrar, Straus and Giroux, 1966), p. 112.

[102]Walter Kerr, *The Decline of Pleasure*, p. 12.

[103]Sinclair Lewis, *Babbitt* (New York: Harcourt, Brace & World, Inc., 1922), p. 230.

[104]E. M. Forster, *A Passage to India* (New York: Harcourt, Brace & World, Inc., 1924), p. 140.

[105]*The Confessions*, Book 13, Chapter 9, p. 341.

[106]Emerson, ''Self-Reliance,'' p. 169.

[107]*Raïssa's Journal*, p. 328.

[108]Whittaker Chambers, *Witness*, p. 147.

[109]Chekhov, ''The Lament,'' *People* (Notre Dame, Indiana: Fides Publishers, Inc., 1968), p. 15.

[110]Shakespeare, *As You Like It*, Act 2, Scene 1, lines 15–18, p. 672.

[111]*The Complete Works of St. Teresa of Jesus*, II, p. 217.

[112]Hermann Hesse, *Siddhartha*, translated by Hilda Rosner (New York: New Directions Publishing Corporation, 1951), p. 107.

[113]Shakespeare, *King Lear*, Act 3, Scene 6, lines 102–105, p. 1007.

[114]John Courtney Murray, *We Hold These Truths* (New York: Sheed and Ward, 1960), p. 317.

[115]Kierkegaard, *Philosophical Fragments*, p. 91.

[116]*The Simone Weil Reader*, p. 181.

[117]Aleksandr Solzhenitsyn, ''A World Split Apart,'' address given at Harvard University, June 1978, found in *Solzhenitsyn at Harvard*, edited by Ronald Berman (Washington, D.C.: Ethics and Public Policy Center), p. 12.

[118]Sobrino, *Christology at the Crossroads*, p. 197.

[119]*The Confessions*, Book 4, Chapter 4, p. 98.

[120]Herman Melville, *Moby Dick* (New York: Modern Library, 1950, p. 477.

[121]C. S. Lewis, *Till We Have Faces*, p. 91.

[122]Statement by John Henry Newman in Meriol Trevor, *Newman: Light in Winter*, p. 367.

[123]Voltaire, *Candide and Other Writings*, p. 188.

[124]Lewis Thomas, *The Lives of a Cell: Notes of a Biology Watcher* (New York: Bantam Books, Inc., 1974), p. 156.

[125]Tennyson, ''Ulysses,'' line 43, in *The Poetic and Dramatic Works of Alfred, Lord Tennyson* (Boston: Houghton Mifflin Company, 1898), p. 88.

[126]Daniel Bell.

[127]Richard Lynch.

[128]Emerson, ''Compensation,'' p. 175.

[129]C. S. Lewis, *Perelandra* (New York: The Macmillan Company, 1944), p. 140.

[130]Carl Sandburg.

[131]*The Simone Weil Reader*, p. 87.

[132]*The Complete Works of St. John of the Cross*, p. 472.

[133]*The Complete Works of St. Teresa of Jesus*, II, p. 103.

[134]Ladislaus Boros, *Hidden God*, p. 42.

[135]Emerson, ''Love,'' p. 215.

[136]C. S. Lewis, *Surprised by Joy*, p. 45.

[137]C. S. Lewis, *Till We Have Faces*, p. 22.

[138]G. K. Chesterton, *The Everlasting Man*, p. 101.

[139]Antoine de Saint-Exupéry, *The Little Prince*, p. 87.

[140]Emerson, ''Art,'' p. 309.

[141]G. K. Chesterton, *The Everlasting Man*, p. 107.

[142]Emerson, ''Experience,'' p. 361.

[143]C. S. Lewis, *The Magician's Nephew* (New York: The Macmillan Compnay, 1954), p. 125.

[144]Paul Horgan, *A Distant Trumpet*, p. 354.

[145]Romano Guardini, *The Living God* (New York: Pantheon, 1957), p. 33.

[146]*The Simone Weil Reader*, p. 51.

[147]*The Complete Works of St. John of the Cross*, p. 537.

[148]Ladislaus Boros, *Hidden God*, p. 12.

[149]Emerson, ''Self-Reliance,'' p. 160.

[150]Paul Horgan, *A Distant Trumpet*, p. 183.

[151]Caryll Houselander, *The Reed of God* (New York: Sheed and Ward, Inc., 1944), p. 31.

[152]Emerson, ''Friendship,'' p. 228.

[153]John Henry Newman, quoted by Meriol Trevor, *Newman: Light in Winter*, p. 540.

[154]*The Simone Weil Reader*, p. 113.

[155]C. S. Lewis, *Surprised by Joy*, pp. 32–33.

[156]Thornton Wilder, *The Bridge of San Luis Rey*, p. 92.

[157]Emerson, ''Friendship,'' p. 236.

[158]George Santayana, quoted in Gardner and Reese, *Know or Listen to Those Who Know*, p. 136.

[159]Emerson, ''Nature,'' p. 410.

[160]Gerald Vann, *St. Thomas Aquinas*, p. 97.

[161]C. S. Lewis, *The Magician's Nephew*, p. 125.

[162]Lawrence Elliott, *I Will Be Called John* (New York: Reader's Digest Press/E. P. Dutton & Company, Inc., 1973), p. 192.

[163]Don Taylor, *Paradise Restored*, Sequence 44, in *Classic Theater*, edited by Sylvan Barnet, Morton Berman, and William Burto (Boston: Little, Brown and Company, 1975), p. 216.

[164]Simone Weil, *Waiting for God* (New York: Harper Colophon Books, 1951), p. 128.

[165]Whittaker Chambers, *Witness*, p. 292.

[166]*Ibid.*, p. 457.

[167]Emerson, ''Spiritual Laws,'' p. 206.

[168]C. S. Lewis, *The Four Loves* (New York: Harcourt, Brace, Jovanovich, Inc., 1960), p. 27.

[169]Meriol Trevor, *Newman: Light in Winter*, p. 606.

[170]Herman Melville, *Moby Dick*, p. 201.

[171]Nathaniel Hawthorne, *The Scarlet Letter*, in Kenneth S. Lynn, *The Scarlet Letter: Text, Sources, Criticism* (New York: Harcourt, Brace & World, Inc., 1961), p. 90.

[172]Ibsen, *Hedda Gabler*, Act 4.

[173]Emerson, ''Power,'' p. 383.

[174]Louis Dupré, *Transcendent Selfhood: The Rediscovery of the Inner Life* (New York: The Seabury Press, 1976), p. 44.

[175]Walter Kerr, *The Decline of Pleasure*, p. 77.

[176]Shakespeare, *King Lear*, Act 2, Scene 4, lines 103–106, p. 999.

[177]Michael Wilson as quoted in Thomas Kane, *The Healing Touch of Affirmation* (Whitinsville, Massachusetts: Affirmation Books, 1976), pp. 51–52.

[178]William Lynch, *The Integrating Mind* (New York: Sheed and Ward, 1962), p. 123.

[179]Norman Cousins.

[180]Robert A. Johnson, *He* (New York: Perennial Library, Harper and Row, Publishers, 1977), p. 37.

[181]Murray Bodo, *Francis: The Journey and the Dream* (Cincinnati: St. Anthony Messenger Press, 1972), p. 129.

[182]C. Harold Dodd, *The Meaning of Paul for Today* (Cleveland: Collins Publishers, 1957), p. 135.

[183]Dante, *The Divine Comedy*, p. 133.

[184]Paul Horgan, *A Distant Trumpet*, p. 225.

[185]Manzoni, *The Betrothed*, p. 258.

[186]C. S. Lewis, *Surprised by Joy*, pp. 16–17.

[187]Dante, *The Divine Comedy*, p. 96.

[188]*Anne Frank: The Diary of a Young Girl*, p. 258.

[189]*The Confessions*, Book 4, Chapter 8, p. 101.

[190]Antoine de Saint-Exupéry, *The Little Prince*, pp. 83–84.

[191]Emerson, "Self-Reliance," p. 157.

[192]C. S. Lewis, *The Screwtape Letters*, p. 68.

[193]C. S. Lewis, *Surprised by Joy*, p. 226.

[194]John Henry Newman, *Apologia Pro Vita Sua*, p. 169.

[195]Dante, *The Divine Comedy*, p. 69.

[196]Emerson, "Nature," p. 419.

[197]John Henry Newman, "Prospects of the Anglican Church," *Essays and Sketches*, I (New York: Longmans, Green and Company, 1948), p. 358.

[198]*Raïssa's Journal*, p. 297.

[199]G. K. Chesterton, *St. Thomas Aquinas* (New York: Sheed and Ward, 1933), p. 153.

[200]Anne Sexton, "The Saints Come Marching In," *The Awful Rowing Toward God* (Boston: Houghton Mifflin Company, 1975), p. 81.

[201]C. S. Lewis, as quoted in Roger Lancelyn Green and Walter Hooper, *C. S. Lewis: A Biography* (New York: Harcourt, Brace, Jovanovich, Inc., 1974), p. 227.

[202]Karl Rahner, "Priest and Poet," *The Word: Readings in Theology* (New York: P. J. Kenedy & Sons, 1964), p. 16.

[203]Emerson, "Self-Reliance," p. 163.

[204]Henri Nouwen, *The Genesee Diary: Report from a Trappist Monastery* (New York: Doubleday & Company, 1976), p. 110.

[205]Murray Bodo, *Francis: The Journey and the Dream*, p. 64.

[206]*The Simone Weil Reader*, p. 44.

[207]*The Complete Works of St. Teresa of Jesus*, I, p. 49.

[208]Sobrino, *Christology at the Crossroads*, p. 158.

[209]François Roustang, S. J., *Growth in the Spirit*, translated by Kathleen Pond (New York: Sheed and Ward, 1963), pp. 71–72.

[210]Julian of Norwich, *Showings*, p. 203.

[211]Johannas B. Metz, *Poverty of Spirit* (Ramsey, New Jersey: Paulist Press, 1968), p. 34.

[212]Thomas Hardy, *The Return of the Native* (New York: The New American Library, 1959), p. 77.

[213]Emerson, "Love," p. 215.

[214]C. S. Lewis, *The Screwtape Letters*, p. 135.

[215]*The Complete Works of St. Teresa of Jesus*, I, p. 296.

[216]Thomas More, *Utopia*, Book 2, translated and edited by Robert Adams (New York: W. W. Norton and Company, Inc., 1978), p. 60.

[217]*Raïssa's Journal*, p. 71.

[218]*The Complete Works of St. John of the Cross*, p. 100.

[219]Walter Bagehot as quoted in Gardner and Reese, *Know or Listen to Those Who Know*, p. 109.

[220]Dante, *The Divine Comedy*, p. 3.

[221]Walter Kerr, *The Decline of Pleasure*, p. 243.

[222]Emerson, "New England Reformers," p. 468.

[223]Meriol Trevor, *Newman: Light in Winter*, p. 158.

[224]Whittaker Chambers, *Witness*, p. 19.

[225]Antoine de Saint-Exupéry, *The Little Prince*, p. 46.

[226]Norman Cousins.

[227]Ladislaus Boros, *Hidden God*, p. 111.

[228]Roustang, *Growth in the Spirit*, p. 125.

[229]Murray, *We Hold These Truths*, p. 69.

[230]Shakespeare, *The Tempest*, Act 2, Scene 1, lines 132–135, p. 1308.

[231]Chesterton, *St. Thomas Aquinas*, p. 92.

[232]Thomas Merton, *The Seven Storey Mountain* (New York: Harcourt, Brace and Company, 1948), p. 372.

[233]C. S. Lewis, *Surprised by Joy*, p. 121.

[234]Emerson, "Friendship," pp. 224–225.

[235]Chesterton, *St. Thomas Aquinas*, p. 165.

[236]Martin Buber, *Pointing the Way*, translated by Maurice S. Friedman (New York: Schocken Books, 1974), p. 198.

[237]Shakespeare, *The Tempest*, Act 5, Scene 1, lines 179–182, p. 1323.

[238]Antoine de Saint-Exupéry, *The Little Prince*, p. 29.

[239]Romano Guardini, *The Life of Faith*, translated by John Chapin (Westminster, Maryland: The Newman Press, 1961), p. 85.

[240]Sobrino, *Christology at the Crossroads*, p. 364.

[241]Emerson, "The American Scholar," p. 50.

[242]Anne Morrow Lindbergh, *Gift from the Sea* (New York: Random House, Inc., 1965), p. 56.

[243]G. K. Chesterton, *Orthodoxy* (New York: Doubleday, Image Books, 1959), p. 17.

[244]Emerson, "Experience," p. 358.

[245]C. S. Lewis, *Out of the Silent Planet*, p. 75.

[246]Dante, *The Divine Comedy*, p. 39.

[247]Raïssa Maritain, *We Have Been Friends Together*, p. 148.

[248]C. G. Jung as quoted by Gardner and Reese, *Know or Listen to Those Who Know*, p. 41.

[249]Walter Kerr, *The Decline of Pleasure*, p. 311.

[250]Lewis Thomas, *The Lives of a Cell*, p. 43.

[251]John Haughey, *The Conspiracy of God* (Garden City: Doubleday, Inc., 1976), pp. 97–98.

[252]François Roustang, *Growth in the Spirit*, p. 171.

[253]*The Complete Works of St. Teresa of Avila*, II, p. 346.

[254]Louis Dupré, *Transcendent Selfhood*, p. 45.

[255]Nouwen, *The Genesee Diary*, p. 152.

[256]Sobrino, *Christology at the Crossroads*, p. 215.

[257]*The Cloud of Unknowing*, edited by William Johnston (New York: Doubleday, Inc., 1973), p. 127.

[258]*The Complete Works of St. Teresa of Jesus*, I, p. 143.

[259]Newman, *Apologia pro Vita Sua*, p. 103.

[260]Voltaire, *Candide and Other Writings*, p. 180.

[261]Jung, *Memories, Dreams, Reflections*, p. 72.

[262]*Beowulf*, lines 1854–1855, p. 60.

[263]*Anne Frank: The Diary of a Young Girl*, p. 274.

[264]John Courtney Murray, *We Hold These Truths*, p. 119.

[265]Emerson, "History," p. 130.

[266]C. S. Lewis, *Till We Have Faces*, p. 96.

[267]Loren Eiseley, *The Night Country*, p. 76.

[268]Chesterton, *The Everlasting Man*, p. 139.

[269]Jung, *Memories, Dreams, Reflections*, pp. 141–142.

[270]Chesterton, *St. Thomas Aquinas*, p. 51.

[271]*The Simone Weil Reader*, p. 160.

[272]Houselander, *The Reed of God*, p. 50.

[273]François Roustang, *Growth in the Spirit*, p. 113.

[274]Thornton Wilder, *The Bridge of San Luis Rey*, p. 112.

[275]C. S. Lewis, *The Great Divorce* (New York: The Macmillan Publishing Company, Inc., 1946), p. 97.

[276]Edna St. Vincent Millay, "Pity me not because the light of day," *The Oxford Book of American Verse* (New York: Oxford University Press, 1950), p. 890.

[277]Hermann Hesse, *Siddhartha*, p. 97.

[278]E. M. Forster, *A Passage to India*, p. 19.

[279]Alessandro Manzoni, *The Betrothed*, p. 123.

[280]Robert Bolt, *A Man for All Seasons*, p. 91.

[281]*The Confessions of St. Augustine*, Book 4, Chapter 14, p. 107.

[282]Emerson, "Friendship," p. 223.

[283]C. S. Lewis, *The Four Loves*, p. 60.

[284]John Henry Newman as quoted by Meriol Trevor, *Newman: The Pillar of the Cloud* (Garden City: Doubleday, 1962), p. 319.

[285]*Ibid.*, p. 474.

[286]John XXIII, as quoted by Lawrence Elliott, *I Will Be Called John*, p. 43.

[287]Teresa of Avila, as quoted by Phyllis McGinley, *Saint-Watching* (New York: Image Books, 1974), p. 19.

[288]*The Confessions of St. Augustine*, Book 6, Chapter 4, p. 138.

[289]Emerson, "Self-Reliance," p. 161.

[290]*The Complete Works of St. Teresa of Jesus*, I, p. 210.

[291]Thomas Merton, *The Seven Storey Mountain*, p. 163.

[292]Herman Melville, *Moby Dick*, p. 112.

[293]Christopher Marlowe, *Edward II*, Act 5, Scene 4, lines 52–53, in *The Plays of Christopher Marlowe* (New York: World Publishing Company, 1962), p. 333.

[294]Dante, *The Divine Comedy*, p. 4.

[295]Emerson, "Friendship," p. 233.

[296]C. S. Lewis, *The Screwtape Letters*, p. 59.

[297]Sidney J. Harris.

[298]*Raïssa's Journal*, p. 28.

[299]C. H. Dodd, *The Meaning of Paul for Today*, p. 121.

[300]Simone Weil, *Waiting for God,* pp. 50–51.

[301]Robert Bolt, *A Man for All Seasons,* p. 81.

[302]C. S. Lewis, *The Four Loves,* p. 169.

[303]Gail Sheehy, *Passages* (New York: E. P. Dutton & Company, 1979), p. 337.

[304]*The Simone Weil Reader,* p. 23.

[305]*Ibid.,* p. 138.

[306]*The Confessions of St. Augustine,* Book 7, Chapter 16, p. 175.

[307]C. S. Lewis, *The Voyage of the Dawn Treader,* p. 157.

[308]Georges Bernanos, *The Diary of a Country Priest,* p. 112.

[309]Paul Horgan, *The Devil in the Desert,* p. 52.

[310]*The Simone Weil Reader,* p. 54.

[311]Alessandro Manzoni, *The Betrothed,* p. 432.

[312]*The Complete Works of St. Teresa of Jesus,* II, p. 315.

[313]*The Simone Weil Reader,* p. 106.

[314]Carl G. Jung, *Memories, Dreams, Reflections,* p. 144.

[315]Robert Bolt, *A Man for All Seasons,* p. 29.

[316]Romano Guardini, *The Life of Faith,* p. 95.

[317]Walter Kerr, *The Decline of Pleasure,* p. 304.

[318]Carl G. Jung, *Memories, Dreams, Reflections,* p. 348.

[319]Emerson, "Compensation," p. 179.

[320]C. S. Lewis, *The Silver Chair* (New York: The Macmillan Company, 1954), p. 187.

[321]Nathaniel Hawthorne, *The Scarlet Letter,* p. 132.

[322]Richard Brinsley Sheridan, *The Rivals,* Act 2, Scene 1, p. 79.

[323]Chekhov, *The Lament,* p. 16.

[324]Alessandro Manzoni, *The Betrothed,* p. 486.

[325]*The Complete Works of St. John of the Cross,* p. 577.

[326]C. S. Lewis, *The Horse and His Boy,* p. 62.

[327]John Henry Newman, as quoted in Meriol Trevor, *Newman: The Pillar of the Cloud,* p. 340.

[328]G. K. Chesterton, *The Everlasting Man,* p. 108.

[329]Nathaniel Hawthorne, *The Scarlet Letter,* p. 110.

[330]Hannah Hurnard, *Hind's Feet on High Places* (Old Tappan, New Jersey: Fleming H. Revell Company, 1973), p. 218.

[331]Maisie Ward, *Caryll Houselander: That Divine Eccentric* (New York: Sheed and Ward, 1962), p. 281.

[332]Julian of Norwich, *Showings,* p. 210.

[333]Teresa of Lisieux, as quoted in François Roustang, *Growth in the Spirit,* p. 60.

[334]Romano Guardini, *The Lord* (Chicago: Henry Regnery Company, 1954), pp. 125–126.

[335]C. S. Lewis, *That Hideous Strength,* p. 139.

[336]C. S. Lewis, *The Voyage of the Dawn Treader,* p. 201.

[337]Loren Eiseley, *The Night Country,* p. 123.

[338]G. K. Chesterton, *The Everlasting Man,* p. 142.

[339]G. K. Chesterton, *St. Thomas Aquinas,* pp. 73–74.

[340]Paul Horgan, *A Devil in the Desert,* p. 25.

[341]C. S. Lewis, *Perelandra,* p. 10.

[342]*Beowulf,* lines 286–287, p. 12.

[343]Emerson, "Power," p. 389.

[344]John Henry Newman, "Prospects of the Anglican Church," *Essays and Sketches,* I, p. 368.

[345] Dante, *The Divine Comedy,* p. 42.

[346] Robert Frost, "A Lone Striker," p. 356.

[347] Voltaire, *Candide and Other Writings,* p. 186.

[348] Shakespeare, *Macbeth,* Act 4, Scene 1, line 143, p. 1046.

[349] Emerson, "Prudence," p. 237.

[350] John Henry Newman, as quoted in Meriol Trevor, *Newman: Light in Winter,* p. 213.

[351] Lord Acton, as quoted by Gardner and Reese, *Know or Listen to Those Who Know,* p. 162.

[352] Carl G. Jung, *Memories, Dreams, Reflections,* p. 222.

[353] Georges Bernanos, *The Diary of a Country Priest,* p. 19.

[354] *Anne Frank: The Diary of a Young Girl,* p. 13.

[355] Emerson, "Literature," pp. 659–660.

[356] C. S. Lewis, *Perelandra,* p. 201.

[357] Donald Taylor, *Paradise Restored,* Sequence 38, in *Classic Theater,* p. 212.

[358] Leo Tolstoy, *War and Peace,* p. 971.

[359] Sinclair Lewis, *Babbitt,* p. 196.

[360] Phyllis McGinley, *Saint-Watching,* p. 29.

[361] Thomas Hardy, *The Return of the Native,* p. 39.

[362] Caryll Houselander, *The Reed of God,* pp. 80–81.

[363] Oliver Goldsmith, *She Stoops to Conquer,* edited by Vincent F. Cooper (New York: Barron's Educational Series, Inc., 1958), p. 98.

[364] Emerson, "Experience," p. 351.

[365] *Meister Eckhart,* translated by Raymond Bernard Blakney (New York: Harper Torchbooks, 1941), p. 11.

SOURCES FOR MONTHLY POEMS

Barbara J. Holt's poems are unpublished. Used with permission of the author.

February: Ruth Mary Fox, "Stripped Tree," *Some Did Return* (Fort Lauderdale, Florida: Wake-Brook House, 1976), p. 111.

March: Emily Dickinson, "We like March—his shoes are Purple," *The Complete Poems of Emily Dickinson*, edited by Thomas H. Johnson (Little, Brown & Co., 1960), #1213, p. 535.

May: Gerard Manley Hopkins, "Spring," *Poems of Gerard Manley Hopkins*, edited by Robert Bridges and W. H. Gardner (New York: Oxford University Press, 1948), p. 71.

June: Sister Maura, S.S.N.D. "We Walk in Miracles," *Walking on Water*. Copyright 1972 by The Missionary Society of St. Paul the Apostle in the State of New York. Used by permission of Paulist Press.

August: Alfred, Lord Tennyson, "Flower in the Crannied Wall," *The Poetic and Dramatic Works of Alfred, Lord Tennyson* (Boston: Houghton, Mifflin Co., 1898), p. 274.

September: Emily Dickinson, "As imperceptibly as Grief," *The Complete Poems of Emily Dickinson*, #1540, pp. 642–643.

October: Gerard Manley Hopkins, "Spring and Fall: to a young child," *Poems of Gerard Manley Hopkins*, p. 94.

November: Robert Frost, "My November Guest," *Complete Poems of Robert Frost* (New York: Henry Holt and Company, 1948), p. 8.

OLD TESTAMENT REFERENCES

Genesis

1:1–5	(8/29)	15:24–31	(10/25)
1:26–31	(8/25)	16:14–23	(12/23)
3:1–24	(1/24)	17:40–58	(7/3)
4:1–16	(3/24)	19:8–10	(2/28)
4:23–24	(1/5)		
5:21–24	(3/7)	**2 Samuel**	
18:1–8	(1/9)	7:1–17	(6/14)
22:1–19	(2/16)	11:1–27	(2/8)
27:1–17	(10/13)	19:1–8	(1/17)
29:9–14	(8/22)		
29:15–19	(5/17)	**Jeremiah**	
37:5–11	(1/22)	1:4–12	(7/26)
37:12–20	(3/30)	18:1–6	(8/28)
		31:31–34	(1/26)

Exodus

		Isaiah	
1:11–14	(5/6)	1:10–20	(8/20)
3:1–6	(6/10)	2:2–5	(4/16)
32:1–6	(12/13)	3:16–24	(10/1)
32:13–14	(10/28)	4:2–6	(7/31)
32:15–16	(12/16)	5:1–4	(10/2)
32:30–35	(12/26)	6:1–9	(9/1)
		9:1–2	(3/9)
Leviticus		41:14–16	(10/16)
26:3–7	(4/18)	42:1–4	(5/15)
		42:14	(5/9)
Deuteronomy		43:1–5	(2/11)
6:4–9	(9/17)		
8:1–6	(2/21)	**1 Kings**	
9:7–14	(1/1)	2:1–11	(3/4)
30:15–20	(4/11)	8:22–40	(8/12)
32:48–52	(3/3)	20:35–43	(10/7)

2 Maccabees

		2 Kings	
7:1–29	(3/2)	1:9–11	(3/23)

Job

		Esther	
3:3–26	(1/18)	2:16–17	(5/20)
29:18–20	(8/23)	4:12–14	(5/14)
37	(7/16)		
38–39	(4/7)	**Ruth**	
		2	(2/7)

1 Samuel

		Wisdom	
1:9–18	(4/4)	2:16–20	(8/3)
15:24–31	(4/6)	6:1–12	(6/21)

7:15–21	(6/29)
9:1–12	(6/11)

Proverbs

1:20–33	(8/14)
3:1–35	(6/9)
8:22–31	(2/26)
9:7–12	(6/17)
14:10	(11/4)
14:20	(6/5)
14:31	(12/3)
14:33	(10/6)
17:11	(6/19)
24:3	(12/5)
31:1–31	(12/21)

Tobit

14:12–15	(3/6)

Micah

6:8	(8/5)

Ezekiel

34:23–31	(4/20)

Ecclesiastes

2:4–11	(5/7)
3:1–6	(7/8)
3:7	(5/12)
5:1–5	(7/25)
10:8–9	(11/26)

Sirach

1:1–10	(8/11)
1:11–20	(10/19)
1:22–24	(9/29)
1:25–40	(10/9)
6:5–17	(6/2)
7:11–12	(11/22)
7:14–15	(11/18)
10:6–18	(9/6)
11:29–34	(11/1)
12:1–7	(8/4)
17:1–4	(8/24)
18:19–29	(10/24)

19:4–12	(7/18)
20:1–8	(11/17)
51:13–38	(8/10)

Hosea

1:2–9	(5/19)
2:1–13	(8/18)

Song of Songs

1:1–4	(6/3)
2:8–3:5	(2/13)
4:1–10	(10/8)
8:5–7	(12/20)

Psalms

1	(4/12)
5	(9/8)
6	(9/7)
14	(10/4)
16:8–11	(3/13)
25	(4/29)
27	(9/26)
28	(7/11)
29	(7/15)
32	(6/15)
37:3–7	(5/29)
38	(8/13)
39	(4/30)
42–43	(1/15)
44:23–26	(5/13)
45:10–17	(5/16)
46:10	(5/10)
52:8–9	(4/17)
65	(11/9)
66	(7/22)
69	(11/25)
71	(9/16)
83	(11/2)
89	(9/12)
91	(11/13)
100	(12/28)
103	(10/27)
104	(5/5)
106	(9/20)
123	(7/6)
126	(4/2)
136	(1/12)
139	(7/28)
145	(6/8)
147	(7/21)
150	(2/24)

NEW TESTAMENT REFERENCES

Matthew

1:16–18	(10/18)	4:13–20	(8/21)	10:29–37	(3/16)
4:1–11	(1/16)	4:30–32	(8/8)	11:29–32	(5/24)
5:1–12	(4/5)	4:30–34	(10/3)	12:1–3	(8/2)
6:5–6	(7/23)	6:17–29	(1/6)	12:4–7	(10/21)
6:7–15	(7/27)	7:1–7	(2/17)	12:22–32	(7/5)
6:25–37	(4/9)	7:1–11	(11/11)	13:6–9	(2/6)
9:9	(9/13)	7:31–37	(11/27)	14:15–24	(3/18)
10:26–31	(9/3)	8:27–33	(6/7)	15:4–7	(11/24)
12:4–7	(6/4)	8:35	(10/23)	15:11–32	(3/19)
12:33–37	(6/24)	9:14–29	(10/15)	16:19–31	(1/30)
12:38–42	(3/27)	9:42–50	(1/31)	17:11–19	(11/16)
13:4–9	(3/25)	10:17–22	(4/14)	18:9–14	(2/23)
14:3–10	(2/5)	10:23–27	(8/26)	19:1–10	(5/27)
14:3–12	(4/13)	10:35–40	(7/2)	21:29–33	(12/24)
14:22–33	(2/15)	11:12–14	(9/22)	22:1–6	(1/28)
14:66–73	(11/3)	13:1–4	(8/27)	22:61–62	(2/14)
16:1–4	(1/25)	14:3–9	(12/30)	24:9–11	(11/19)
16:17–20	(8/27)	14:17–21	(12/25)	24:13–35	(2/2)
16:21–23	(6/18)	14:32–42	(1/27)		
18:12–14	(9/23)	15:1–15	(10/20)	**John**	
18:21–35	(11/7)	15:33–39	(7/13)	1:1–18	(7/20)
19:16–22	(12/2)	15:40–41	(4/23)	1:35–51	(2/22)
19:27–30	(3/31)			2:13–22	(1/3)
20:1–6	(5/1)	**Luke**		3:1–21	(7/12)
20:20–23	(9/5)	1:11–22	(3/11)	4:1–10	(1/19)
21:12–17	(3/20)	1:26–38	(4/25)	4:15–26	(10/31)
23:33–36	(1/29)	2:36–38	(7/7)	4:27–30	(12/1)
25:31–46	(2/9)	2:51–52	(1/23)	6:1–15	(6/26)
26:14–16	(12/14)	4:42	(12/12)	6:26–27	(9/21)
26:38–43	(5/31)	5:4–7	(5/4)	6:52–66	(11/12)
26:56	(10/17)	5:12–24	(9/2)	7:45–52	(3/26)
27:3–10	(2/3)	5:27–28	(8/9)	8:3–11	(1/21)
28:16–20	(6/27)	6:6–11	(6/20)	11:32–37	(3/17)
		6:36–38	(9/27)	12:1–8	(8/30)
Mark		6:43–45	(11/15)	12:37–43	(6/30)
1:35–39	(6/16)	7:36–50	(9/28)	13:1–15	(12/11)
2:1–12	(6/22)	8:11–15	(12/9)	13:21–30	(8/19)
2:13–14	(5/25)	8:43–56	(5/18)	14:23	(9/24)
3:13–19	(9/30)	9:24	(3/29)	15:1–6	(6/23)
3:22–30	(9/18)	9:28–36	(2/20)	15:7–12	(10/29)
4:10–12	(5/28)	9:51–56	(1/4)	15:13–17	(6/6)

16:16–19	(7/9)	9:1–19	(1/10)
16:22–24	(3/10)	15:8–12	(12/27)
17:24–26	(6/13)	15:36–40	(10/12)
18:1–11	(3/15)	16:16–24	(4/24)
19:25–27	(11/28)		
20:1–10	(10/5)	**1 Timothy**	
20:11–18	(10/14)	3:1–7	(10/22)
20:19–21	(4/21)	4:16	(11/21)
21:1–14	(12/31)	6:11–16	(1/13)
21:15–19	(6/1)		
21:24–25	(12/18)	**Galatians**	

Romans

		1:6–10	(2/19)
		1:17–18	(5/11)
1:8–15	(9/9)	1:19–24	(12/19)
2:18–32	(9/11)	2:19–21	(4/8)
5:1–11	(1/8)	4:3–7	(3/21)
6:5–7	(8/6)	5:19–21	(1/20)
7:14–25	(2/25)		
8:18–27	(2/1)	**Philippians**	
8:28–30	(9/14)	1:21–26	(3/5)
8:31–39	(4/1)	2:6–11	(7/17)
9:14–24	(4/26)	4:4–9	(3/14)
11:33–36	(1/14)	4:10–13	(11/29)
12:9–13	(2/12)		
12:14–21	(4/15)	**2 Corinthians**	
13:8–10	(10/30)	4:7–12	(4/10)
13:11–14	(7/10)	5:1–6	(7/29)
		5:6–10	(3/1)

Ephesians

		8:9	(6/28)
		12:1–6	(5/23)
1:3–14	(4/3)	12:7–10	(4/22)
2:3–6	(1/2)	13:11–13	(10/11)
3:14–21	(2/27)		
4:17–32	(12/15)	**Phileman**	
5:1–20	(2/4)	1:1	(9/10)
6:14–17	(4/19)	1:8–21	(8/7)

1 Corinthians

		Colossians	
1:4–9	(9/19)	1:3–14	(3/22)
1:10–16	(1/7)	1:15–20	(8/31)
3:5–9	(5/2)	2:6–8	(8/16)
12:4–11	(1/11)	3:5–11	(7/1)
13:1–13	(7/19)	3:12–14	(5/30)
15:50–53	(12/29)	4:2–6	(3/28)

Acts

		1 Thessalonians	
		2:17–20	(6/25)
2:14–36	(12/7)	5:1–3	(7/14)
2:42–47	(12/22)	5:15	(9/25)
4:1–22	(9/4)		
7:1–60	(2/18)	**2 Thessalonians**	
9:1–19	(10/26)	1:3–11	(7/24)

3:6–12   (5/3)

1 John
1:1–4   (3/8)
1:8–10   (11/6)
2:3–11   (9/15)
3:17–20   (12/8)
4:7–11   (2/10)
5:5–12   (11/14)
5:18–21   (8/15)

James
1:2–12   (4/27)
1:13–18   (7/4)
1:19–27   (11/10)
3:1–13   (5/8)

1 Peter
1:3–9   (11/23)
1:8–9   (5/26)
1:22–24   (10/10)
2:1–3   (8/1)
3:8–12   (12/10)
4:12–19   (4/28)

Jude
1:8–10   (11/20)

2nd Peter
2:11–22   (11/5)

Hebrews
5:1–10   (11/30)
11:1–3   (11/8)

Revelations
1:1–3   (12/17)
1:9–20   (5/22)
5:6–12   (7/30)
12:1–17   (6/12)
19:7   (3/12)
19:11–21   (12/4)
21:1–8   (5/21)
22:1–15   (12/6)